The Art and Politics of Thomas Nast

Mr. Thomas Nast

[Photographed by Brady]

The Art and Politics
of
THOMAS NAST

Morton Keller

New York
OXFORD UNIVERSITY PRESS
1968

To Dexter Perkins

Preface

It is time that the art of Thomas Nast came to the attention of a public who knows him only tangentially and piecemeal. My first intention is to present what I judge to be the best of Nast's immensely rich and evocative body of work. America's greatest political cartoonist published more than three thousand drawings over the course of his career. The great majority (and the best) of them appeared in *Harper's Weekly* between 1862 and 1885. It is from this source that the cartoons here reproduced have come.

To a considerable degree these drawings speak for themselves. It is true that they depict ephemeral men and events, but their inventive power is as evident today as it was a century ago. Nast's was a rare talent at a time when American art showed little vitality. The most important American critic of the time, James Jackson Jarves, observed in *The Art-Idea* (1864), when Nast's career was just beginning, that here was "an artist of uncommon originality of conception, freedom of manner, lofty appreciation of national ideas and action, and a large

---

* Part of the force of Nast's cartoons came from their size. His *Harper's* cover drawings measured approximately 9⅛ x 10¾ inches; inside full-page cartoons, 9⅛ x 13⅝; double-page spreads, 20½ x 13⅝. They have been reproduced here at two-thirds their original size. Smaller cartoons have been reduced to eighty per cent of original size.

artistic instinct." In the great outpouring that was to come, Nast more than lived up to Jarves's critical estimate.

But Nast has more than artistic importance. His work is a richly detailed record of a distinctive period in the American past. No one better expressed the national mood of optimism in the American future that came on the heels of the Civil War. And no one better conveyed the painful disillusionment with the public order that spread over important areas of public opinion during the 1870's and the early 1880's.

Unlike his contemporary, Honoré Daumier, Nast had little to say about the social mores of his time. Indeed, he fully shared the values of the comfortable, godly farmers and townsmen who composed his *Harper's Weekly* audience. His great theme was the interplay of men and issues that made up the flow of party controversy. He and his audience viewed politics as a deeply meaningful form of expression, a receptacle for their profoundest fears, beliefs, expectations. "In a free government," said *Harper's Weekly* editor George W. Curtis, "parties are not only organizations to secure certain policies— they are also representations of certain tendencies and principles in human nature and society." Nast's cartoons were powerful—and influential—because his was the truest voice of post-Civil War Republicanism.

During his most productive years Nast created a gallery of symbols and caricatures that for long would have a prominent place in the American political imagination. He created or popularized the figures of the Tammany tiger, the Republican elephant, the Democratic donkey, the workingman's cap and dinner pail, the Rag Baby of inflationist sentiment. In his powerful exposé of the Tweed Ring he fixed once and for all the stereotype of the corrupt city boss; in his terrible anti-Catholic cartoons he tapped dark fears in the American Protestant consciousness.

To appreciate fully Nast's potent and imaginative art, it is necessary to have some understanding of the political milieu from which it came.

Our sense of post-Civil War American public life has been shaped by eloquent and perceptive contemporaries—Henry Adams, E.L. Godkin, Mark Twain—whose disillusion was quick and easy because it was intensely personal or because they had no great expectations to begin with. But Nast's work evokes something else: the idealism and optimism that in fact had a prominent place in post-Civil War public life. The surge of belief that society can be quickly and thoroughly reformed, and then the angry, wasting disillusionment that comes when unrealistic hopes run afoul of stubborn social realities, is a phenomenon all too familiar in our own time. This drama of political expectation and disenchantment was played out with special poignancy in the years after the Civil War.

The political tawdriness of the Gilded Age came only after a time of striking public vigor. The most dramatic evidence of that boldness was the cluster of political acts that followed Negro emancipation: the 14th and 15th amendments to the Constitution, the Civil Rights Acts of 1866 and 1875. They reflected a view of American citizenship that would not again be an important force in public life until our own time. But the civil rights legislation of the postwar years was only the most dramatic expression of a more general political ideology: the ideology of Radical Republicanism. *Harper's Weekly* summed up the Radical Republican creed in 1870: "A hearty faith in the great principles of popular government, a generous hospitality toward new views and constant progress, a practical perception of the close relation between morals and politics, a deep conviction of the vital necessity of intelligence to a true republic, will generally lead a man to act with the Republican party." By the same token the Democratic party was more than the political opposition; it was the repository of specific—and undesirable—social characteristics: disloyalty, Negrophobia, reaction. "Which party," *Harper's* asked, "everywhere depends upon the ignorance and prejudice of the voters? Which is strongest in the slums of great cities, and in the rural parts of the Union where there are fewest schools?"

The Radical Republican spirit did not last long, nor were its achievements substantial or permanent. A politics of organization and place-serving submerged Radical Republican idealism and social purpose. Renascent racism, the enervating depression of the 1870's, the demands of a burgeoning industrial capitalism soon reduced those ideals to the empty rhetoric of the politicos.

Nast commented brilliantly on the decay of the Radical Republican ethos, as he had done on its flowering. But when the transformation was complete, so ended his ability to portray meaningfully the public life of his time. The spirit of Radical Republicanism was the ideological stimulus for the most powerful and sustained political commentary in our history. When that spirit faded, so did the force and fire of Nast's art.

Cambridge, Massachusetts   M.K.
January 1968

Contents

The Art and Politics of Thomas Nast

I
The Art of Thomas Nast

The art of social commentary to which the work of Thomas Nast belongs is the special property of the post-Renaissance Western World. We think we can identify the first caricaturist: that is to say, the first artist to devote himself to the comic distortion of identifiable men. This was the Italian Annibale Carracci, who belonged to a Bolognese family of painters that flourished at the beginning of the seventeenth century. The word "caricature" comes not from the family's name but from the Italian *caricare*, to charge or to overcharge—suggestive of the compressed force of expression that is peculiar to the technique. Carracci recognized its latent power. Supposedly he observed: "Is not the caricaturist's task exactly the same as the classical artist's? Both see the lasting truth beneath the surface of mere outward appearance. . . . A good caricature, like every work of art, is more true to life than reality itself."

The development of caricature and other devices of satiric social art meant that a compelling form of artistic expression had come into being. The artist as social commentator has awesome weapons— wit, symbolism, animalism—to direct at men and institutions. Satiric art has much in common with fundamental manifestations of the unconscious such as wit and dreams. The distortions of great caricature, the transferences wrought by animal symbolism, the use of

3

satiric humor, are among the most potent devices by which one man can strike at another. They touch upon deep fears of and belief in the power to wreak harm upon an adversary by representation, by distortion, by imagery. The art historian E. H. Gombrich did not exaggerate when he observed that "the cartoonist can *mythologize the world by physiognomizing it.*" At his height Nast wielded what he recognized to be a "terrible" power over his political contemporaries. Boss Tweed of New York, Nast's most notable victim, in his own way recognized the force of the artist's work when he said: "I don't care a straw for your newspaper articles, my constituents don't know how to read, but they can't help seeing them damned pictures."

In the eighteenth and nineteenth centuries, two great schools of graphic social commentary fixed the modern stylistic boundaries of the form. They provided the immediate artistic background for the work of Thomas Nast.

The first of these schools flourished in eighteenth- and early nineteenth-century England. A public now existed eager to engage vicariously in political life by patronizing an artistic commentary of great vigor—and great scurrility. The Hanoverian England that welcomed the verbal satire of Pope and Swift supported a rich art of caricature. William Hogarth's searing observations on the social mores of the 1730's and the 1740's, and on the politics of the reign of George II, set the style. George Townshend in the 1750's concentrated on affairs of state, and made political caricature a characteristically English art form. Sufficient civil liberty existed for bitterly anti-Establishmentarian work to have a wide public circulation. It became fashionable for country houses to have their folios of maledictory engravings and broadsides.

The great age of English political drawing came during the climactic turn-of-the-century struggle with France. The sustained crisis of those years focused public attention as never before upon public men and public affairs. Artists appeared who took full advantage of the opportunity, chief among them James Gillray and Thomas Rowlandson. Gillray depended heavily upon allegory and fantasy; but he is most notable for his representations—obscene, bloated, vigorous—of prominent public men and of the British citizenry. Rowlandson in the early 1800's spurred English patriotism with his indictments of Napoleon and his policies.

As the passions of the Napoleonic years subsided, English political art lost its bite. Static and restrained statements were the fashion in the Victorian epoch, except for such special times of stress as the Crimean War. *Punch*, founded in 1841, was the great vehicle of the new respectability. Its drawings were the first in a periodical to be called "cartoons"—with the connotation of insipidity that the word now carried. The work of Sir John Tenniel and Sir Bernard Partridge, which dominated the magazine's pages through the last half of the nineteenth century, typified the gentility that had come to English graphic art.

Nast learned much from the British graphic artists of his time. He was directly influenced by John Leech and Tenniel of *Punch*, and by the painter and book illustrator John Gilbert. But the best of his work was closer in spirit to the great school of nineteenth-century French drawing. Post-Napoleonic France was wracked by an endless, unresolved struggle between the republican and monarchical halves of the nation. Out of this perpetual turmoil emerged a brilliant art of political and social commentary. Its first great medium, in the 1830's, was a group of journals—the weekly *La Caricature*, the daily *Charivari*, the *Journal pour Rire*—edited by the journalist and caricaturist Charles Philipon. Later in the century Henri Rochefort provided a comparable outlet in *La Lanterne*.

The major figure in this school was, of course, Honoré Daumier. It also included Grandville (whose work has been found appropriate to the pages of the *New York Review of Books*), Gavarni, and Cham. Philipon himself contributed a notable representation of Louis Philippe as *la poire*—the ineluctably bourgeois pear—that would serve Daumier as well, and that seems to have inspired one of Nast's representations of Tweed. (116)

The work of Daumier and his contemporaries had force, elegance, wit—and a passionate commitment to a cause. This was something new to political art. The drawings of Gillray and Rowlandson had no particular message beyond a generalized distaste for their subjects; they espoused no great ideas. But the French caricaturists criticized because they defended—the Republic, liberty, secularism. Their social commitment and their Romantic aesthetic went hand in hand. Art and politics were united in social purpose as well as in subject matter. Mere observation was not enough; engagement was all. Courbet's injunction to make a living art found its echo in one of the few statements attributed to Daumier: "One must be of one's time."

5

Nast's style derived more from the finely delineated engravings of the English cartoonists than from the softened, subtle shadings of the French lithographers. But in spirit he was one with the French Romantics. His commitment to the more perfect Union was as passionate as Daumier's devotion to Liberty and the Republic.

It is necessary to see Nast against the background of a transatlantic art of social commentary, for he could draw on no rich tradition of American graphic satire or caricature. American political drawings appeared in the mid-eighteenth century, and were numerous enough thereafter; but they were crude and uninspired creations. Until the advent of Nast the form remained encased in the conventions of the eighteenth-century English cartoon: stiff, amateurishly drawn, over-burdened with verbiage and detail.

The conditions of American life were responsible for this laggard development. The audience for political etchings and lithographs was limited. A vast, sprawling, essentially rural country did not provide a ready market for political art. No metropolis—no London or Paris —existed to spur and absorb such work.

The most notable American political art in the half-century before the Civil War celebrated the rise of American nationalism or commented on the foibles of party politics. The female figure of Columbia and the male figure of Uncle Sam or Brother Jonathan were products of the patriotic enthusiasm stirred by the War of 1812. At about the same time there appeared that mythical beast the Gerrymander, a representation of a Massachusetts district shaped to meet the political needs of Governor Elbridge Gerry's party.

But the issues that most passionately engaged the American people —the Revolution and independence, and then, almost a century later. the controversy over slavery and states' rights—evoked great words, not great pictures. Congressional orations, pamphlets, books, and speeches sped over the vast country far more rapidly and less expensively than could etchings, lithographs, or engravings. Nor did the commanding issues of the time readily lend themselves to pictorial representation. Confrontations of ideas—liberty against empire, national union against state sovereignty, freedom against slavery— demanded sustained, detailed, ever-changing elaboration. These the words of a Paine or a Jefferson, a Webster or a Calhoun could best provide.

Developments in the 1850's made possible the emergence of an art

6

of social and political commentary. *Frank Leslie's Illustrated Newspaper*, the first successful pictorial magazine in the United States, appeared in 1855. *Harper's Weekly*, which was to serve as Nast's great medium, followed in 1857. By 1860 *Leslie's* had a circulation of over 160,000, *Harper's* almost 100,000; each copy had many readers. During the same years Currier & Ives lithographs—sometimes treating political topics—habituated large numbers of Americans to the pictorial representation of ideas and events.

The Civil War provided these new outlets of American graphic art with their first great theme. And in Thomas Nast an artist appeared with gifts of technique, imagination, and feeling powerful enough to reach and move the vast audience now at hand.

Nast was born in a military barracks in the German Palatinate on September 27, 1840. His father was a musician in a Bavarian regimental band. As was the case with so many of his countrymen, the elder Nast was drawn to America by the dual temptations of social freedom and economic opportunity. He sent his family to New York in 1846, and joined them soon after.

Thomas Nast's Germanic origins figured in his work. From his native folklore he extracted one of his lasting creations: the classic Santa Claus of the American imagination, a round cheery dispenser of gifts exuding, as one critic has said, "a Biedemeier *Gemütlichkeit*." Ideas as well as images were part of Nast's family inheritance. The son of a man who in spirit was a "forty-eighter," he was exposed from his earliest days to the nationalism, the secularism, the belief in progress that were the major elements of mid-nineteenth-century German liberalism.

As Nast came of age he moved among people and experienced events that reinforced the political and social assumptions of his family inheritance. The woman he married in 1861, Sarah Edwards, was a cousin of the biographer James Parton. She and her friends—who became Nast's friends—were of the genteel middle class, especially responsive to romantic, liberal, and nationalistic ideals. Nast long remembered the triumphant visit of the Hungarian nationalist leader Louis Kossuth to New York in 1853. In 1860 he accompanied Garibaldi on his march of national liberation through Sicily and southern Italy, portraying for New York and London journals one of the great adventures of romantic nationalism. He was less directly exposed to the prewar antislavery movement, but he saw John Brown's funeral in

December 1859 and was moved by a eulogy of Brown delivered soon after by Wendell Phillips.

The beginning of Nast's artistic career is coterminous with that of American illustrated journalism. He was a staffer (at the age of 15) on *Leslie's Illustrated* in the early days of that magazine's existence. Thus from the first he was exposed to a mass-circulation journalism whose distinctive qualities—the immediacy and primacy of news, the importance of the lurid and the sensational, the uses of exposure and reform—significantly shaped his work. At *Leslie's,* and then from 1858 to 1862 as a free-lancer for the other important illustrated journals of the time—*Harper's Weekly,* the *New York Illustrated News*—Nast schooled himself in a hectic, vital pictorial journalism. He portrayed the tumultuous life of the metropolis, and covered events of popular interest such as the Heenan-Sayers heavyweight fight in England. He had a hand in a *Leslie's* campaign against the sale of swill milk from diseased cows, and commented on the conditions of New York tenements. His first drawing for *Harper's* was an ironic examination of police corruption.

The conditions of illustrated weekly journalism affected Nast's artistic technique as much as it did the content of his work. His great medium was the wood-block engraving. Not until the 1880's, when his best work was behind him, were his cartoons reproduced by a photochemical engraving process. Nast's first important drawings, comments on the Civil War, relied appropriately enough on somber, fluid tones of gray and black. After the war, when he turned to a vigorous political commentary, his work became notable for the sharpness and clarity of its line.

But the significance of Nast's art lies more in what he had to say than in how he went about saying it. "The idea is the thing," a critic has observed of his work. There is a notable correlation between the quality of Nast's drawings and the force of the conviction that lies behind them. When he is engaged in causes about which he deeply cares, then we see the "stark, focused style" of his artistic peak. When his passion is spent, and his commitments are muddled—as was the case after the mid-'seventies—his work declines to a level no better than that of many of his contemporaries.

The art of Thomas Nast is most of all a remarkably evocative response to a dramatic period in American public life. Just as English and French political art flourished in times of extraordinary stress, so did Nast derive his strength from the nation's greatest crisis. He had a special receptivity to the most powerful public emotions of his time. It was this that gained him his vast and responsive audience; that stoked the fires of his artistic vigor and imagination; that lifted much of his work out of the realm of the evanescent. And because Americans a century ago addressed themselves to public problems many of which are still a part of our lives, Nast's art speaks with force and relevance today.

II
Civil War

Thomas Nast's first opportunity to influence American sentiment came with the Civil War. His commentary on that struggle is an evocative record of its development into a contest between opposing ideologies. At the same time his work contributed largely to the appearance of a Northern sentiment that made the preservation of the Union and the end of slavery inseparable causes.

The outbreak of violence at first seemed a calamitous accident, to be ended as quickly as possible and the old order of things restored. *Harper's Weekly* shared the prevailing viewpoint in 1861 and 1862. Its drawings and editorials were indifferent or hostile to the cause of abolition. The magazine resisted the view that the war might serve as an instrument of social change.

Indeed, much of the early Northern war effort was in the hands of men and organizations who had their own, often limited sense of how the struggle should be carried on. These were the days of ninety-day volunteers; of colorfully dressed Zouaves; of the all-but-private regiments of ambitious politicians; of General George McClellan, who sympathized more than a little with the social views of his Southern foes and considered his commander in chief "nothing more than a well meaning baboon." This was the time, too, of assertive, independent-minded state governors—John Andrew of Massachusetts, Andrew G. Curtin of Pennsylvania, Oliver P. Morton of Indiana—who raised troops, supplies, and money with magnificent disregard for the direction and the authority of the central government. Andrew wrote in September 1862: "Besides doing my proper work, I am sadly but firmly trying to help organize some movement,

11

if possible to save the Prest. from the infamy of ruining his country."

But as the war dragged on, and deepened in ferocity, changes began to occur in the way in which it was fought and, more profoundly, in the way in which it was perceived. Helter-skelter voluntarism gave way to a more centrally directed war effort. Power came increasingly into the hands of Lincoln, Secretary of War Stanton, and the Joint Congressional Committee on the Conduct of the War. The hardened, drably uniformed regulars of Grant and Sherman became the prototype for the Northern armies; and the remorseless strategies of these generals made the war a grim struggle of human and material attrition.

Most of all, the accumulating years of war wrought a change in Northern sentiment. In order to justify the length and cost of the struggle, a new view of the war took hold: one in which more than the restoration of the Union was at stake. The bulk of Northern public opinion came to accept the view that the war in fact was a struggle over the perpetuation of Negro slavery, a confrontation of opposing views on the nature of government and society in America.

Nast reported pictorially on the great crisis of the Union from its earliest days. As a free-lancer for the leading illustrated weeklies he contributed drawings of Lincoln's March 1861 inauguration and the early departure of Northern regiments. In the summer of 1862 he became a staff artist for *Harper's Weekly*. For that journal he portrayed numerous wartime events: the Confederate guerilla leader John Morgan sacking a village; McClellan making the rounds of the Army of the Potomac; the battles of Antietam, Vicksburg, Gettysburg; the New York City draft riots.

The drawings of Nast and other staff artists (including Winslow Homer) and the editorials of George W. Curtis made *Harper's Weekly* the most important organ of information and opinion in the wartime North. Never before had a great event been conveyed pictorially as well as verbally to so vast an audience. The war as seen through the eyes of the *Harper's* artists became the closest approximation of the sight and sense of the conflict for hundreds of thousands of Northerners.

Nast soon moved to a different sort of statement. "The War in the Border States" (1) and "The Result of War—Virginia in 1863" (2) did not pretend to describe specific events. Rather they were imaginative statements on the grim and terrible nature of the war itself. The massive popular response to these drawings suggests that they tapped a deep public desire to view the war in terms beyond those of literal representation.

While Nast vividly portrayed the war as tragedy, he found a means of offering his audience a compensatory sense of purpose, of justification for all the pain and loss. His commentary on the cause of Emancipation (3) and a series of allegorical celebrations of national holidays (4, 5, 6, 7, 8) caught—and heightened—the mix of patriotism, religiosity, and elevated moral purpose that gave important elements of Northern opinion the will to see the war through to its bloodied, weary end. These works, for all their rodomontade, deeply moved—and inspired—their audience. As Nast's cousin-in-law James Parton later put it: "From a roving lad with a swift pencil for sale, he had become a patriot artist, burning with the enthusiasm of the time." His drawings, said Parton, were "powerful emblematic pictures . . . as much the expression of heartfelt conviction as Mr. Curtis' most impassioned editorials, or Mr. Lincoln's Gettysburg speech."

Such comparisons were not far-fetched. The impact of Nast's "emblematic pictures" was enormous. Grant said of him: "He did as much as any man to preserve the Union and bring the war to an end." More prosaically, Lincoln called Nast "our best recruiting sergeant. His . . . cartoons have never failed to arouse enthusiasm and patriotism, and have always seemed to come just when those articles were getting scarce." The Union League Club of New York honored Nast in 1869 for wartime work that "caught up and reflected, and at the same time strengthened the popular sentiment in favor of the Union and of Equal Rights for All." A testimonial from a group of Army and Navy officers in 1879 recalled "the patriotic use he has made of his rare abilities as the artist of the people."

The climax of the North's emotional response to the Civil War came in the conflict's incredible final days. The sequence of events that included Lee's surrender at Appomattox on Palm Sunday (9) and the assassination of Lincoln on Good Friday (10) had an impact on Nast's strained and wearied audience that is difficult to exaggerate. A great outpouring in the churches on Easter Sunday—"Black Easter" —heard sermons that rang all possible changes on the juxtaposition of holy days and portentous events. The Lincoln funeral procession from Washington to Springfield was the occasion for a final outpouring of emotion by a sorely tried people. Nast caught the national mood with fervid apotheoses of the martyred President and the triumphant Union (11, 12). This was the generation—and the sentiment —to which Nast would always speak; the time which, in a sense, he would never leave.

THE WAR IN TH

January 17, 1863

The War in the West.

[2]

July 18, 1863

The Result of War—Virginia in 1863.

EMANCI

January 24, 1863

The Emancipation of the Negroes, January, 1863—
The Past and the Future.

THANKSGIVING DAY.

THE NAVY.

LINCOLN.

WASHINGTON.

THE ARMY.

THE UNION ALTAR.

COUNTRY.

EMANCIPATION.

TOWN.

AND

THANKSGIVING-DAY, NOVEMBER 26, 1863.

December 5, 1863

[4]

R'S DAY

SOUTH

January 2, 1864

GOING TO THE WAR.

IN THE FIELD.

IN THE HOSPITAL.

IN CHURCH.

RETURNING FROM THE WAR.

ON BOARD.

AROUND THE DEAD.

IN CAMP.

RIGHTS.

July 16, 1864

The Fourth of July, 1864.

THANKSGIVING-DAY

THANK GOD FOR MARYLAND FREEING HER SLAVES.

IN EUROPE.

IN THE FIELD.

UNITE

BLESSED AF

NOVEMBER 24, 1864.

THANK GOD FOR OUR UNION VICTORIES.

IN REBELDOM.

STAND.

Th. Nast.

PEACE MAKERS.

ON BOARD.

December 3, 1864

VICTORY HOLDING OUT THE OLIVE BRANCH TO SUBMISSION

THE UNION CHRI

PEACE ON EARTH A

UNCONDITIONAL SURRENDER

THE HOME TOAST GOD B

[8]

CHRISTMAS DINNER.

GOODWILL TOWARD MEN.

THE RETURN OF THE PRODIGAL SON

THE DOOR HAS BEEN FOR A FULL YEAR OPEN TO ALL

THE PRESIDENT'S MESSAGE

LAY DOWN YOUR ARMS AND YOU WILL BE WELCOME

SOLDIERS AND SAILORS

December 31, 1864

THE SAVIOR'S ENTRY INTO JERUSALEM

WE HOLD OUT THE OLIVE BRANCH TO OUR ERRING AND MISGUIDED BRETHREN OF THE SOUTHERN STATES, AND PLEDGE TO ALL OF THEM WHO ARE LOYAL A HEARTY WELCOME TO ALL THE BENEFITS OF OUR FREE REPUBLIC.

PALM

WE RECOGNIZE HIS HAND

AND HIS KIND PROVIDENCE IN BRINGING THIS NATION SO NEAR TO

TRIUMPHANT END OF THIS MIGHTY CONTEST FOR FREEDOM AND GOOD GOVERNMENT

LIBERTY

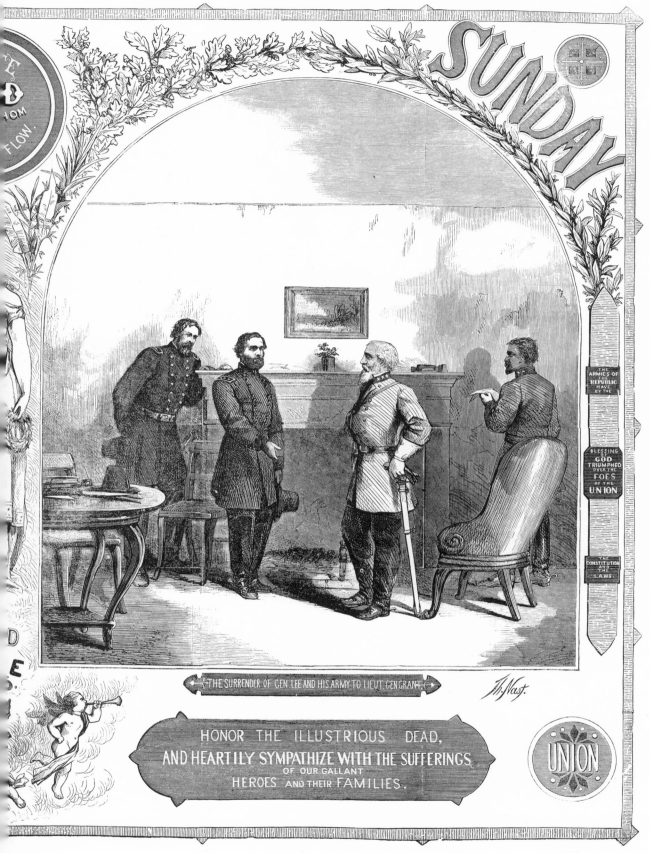

SUNDAY

THE ARMIES OF THE REPUBLIC HAVE BY THE

BLESSING OF GOD TRIUMPHED OVER THE FOES OF THE UNION

THE CONSTITUTION AND THE LAWS

→ THE SURRENDER OF GEN. LEE AND HIS ARMY TO LIEUT. GEN. GRANT ←

Th. Nast.

HONOR THE ILLUSTRIOUS DEAD,
AND HEARTILY SYMPATHIZE WITH THE SUFFERINGS
OF OUR GALLANT
HEROES AND THEIR FAMILIES.

UNION

May 20, 1865

April 29, 1865

Abraham Lincoln,

OUR MARTYRED PRESIDENT.

APRIL 1ST 1865.

OUR SAVIOUR.

THY WILL BE DONE.

VICTORY AND DEATH.

DEATH LEVELS ALL THINGS IN HIS MARCH,
NOUGHT CAN RESIST HIS MIGHTY STRENGTH
THE PALACE PROUD.—TRIUMPHAL ARCH,
SHALL METE THEIR SHADOWS LENGTH

MARVE.

VICTORY.

EUROPE AND AMERICA.

DEATH.

June 10, 1865

[11]

REJOICING OVER UNION VICTORIES.

THE REBELS SURRENDERING THEIR ARMS.

THE CONQUERING TROD.

THE ONLY NATIONAL DEBT WE OWE THAT WE CAN PAY IS THE DEBT WE OWE TO THE VICTORIOUS UNION SOLDIERS AND SAILORS

NAVY

ARMY

ANTIETAM.
CEDAR CREEK.
RINGGOLD.
RAPPAHANNOCK.
GAINES'S MILLS.
SAVAGE STATION.
SPOTSYLVANIA COURT HOUSE.

CULPEPER.
CHICKAHOMINY.
CHANCELLORSVILLE.
FAIR OAKS.
FIVE FORKS.
WHITE OAK ROAD.
MALVERN HILL.

OUR ARMS VICTORIOUS.

HONOR TO THE BRAVE.
GIVE ME THE DEATH OF THOSE
WHO FOR THEIR COUNTRY DIE

VICTORY DEARLY WON.

HOMEWARD BOUND.

HOMEWARD MARCH.

Th. Nast.

June 24, 1865

[12]

III

Reconstruction

The divisions within American society that had sustained so bloody a civil war did not disappear in April 1865. It is true that the Confederate South no longer existed as a political entity. But the political ideas that gave it birth survived—and not in the South alone. A passion for white supremacy and for supine and localized government, a hatred of the complex of nationalism, moral purpose, and liberal humanitarianism that underlay the Union war effort remained conspicuous themes in American public life.

Those who were so committed generally found their political home, during the war and after, in the Democratic party. Most of the white South fell into this category, of course; but so did substantial Northern groups as well. Negrophobic city workingmen—especially the Irish—stood bitterly opposed to the Protestant culture around them and to the Republican party that spoke for it. Large numbers of other Americans in the lower North and the border states who had failed to take fire from the cause of the Union or of antislavery, or who persisted in their familial party loyalties, remained Democrats.

On the other side stood the bulk of popular sentiment in the great sweep of the North from New England to Kansas and Nebraska. This political alliance—the heart of the Republican party—was bound together by economic, religious and ethnic ties. For the most part it was middle class, Protestant, native-born. But in the late 'sixties it shared something else as well: the idea of the triumphant postwar Nation as a force for social justice. Nationalism, liberalism, social reform, and economic development were among the most compelling ideas of the mid-nineteenth century Western world. They found a potent political medium in the Republican party of the Civil War era.

The politics of wartime and of Reconstruction were played out on the battlefield occupied by these opposing forces in American life. The imagery of war is proper here. Politics in these years often seemed to be an inversion of Clausewitz's maxim: to be the continuation of war by other means. The terms that the opposing forces applied to themselves and to each other—Radical, Jacobin; Conservative, Bourbon—suggest the ideological intensity of postwar political life. Radical Republicanism and Conservative Democracy confronted each other not as place- and power-seeking organizations alone, but as the embodiments of opposing ideologies.

National politics set the pace and form of this confrontation. Its milestones were the Lincoln-McClellan presidential election of 1864; the struggle between Andrew Johnson, wedded to the precepts of Conservatism, and a Republican-dominated Congress committed increasingly to the principles of Radicalism; the triumph of Radical Reconstruction; and the Grant-Seymour election of 1868. These were the events that furnished the material for Thomas Nast's declaration of faith as a Radical Republican.

Nast first turned his attention to political themes in the wartime election of 1864. In spirit his commentary was indistinguishable from his work on the war. It is notable that his 1864 political cartoons did not dwell on the figure of Abraham Lincoln, or on Lincoln's Democratic opponent George McClellan, but on the Union Republican and Democratic parties as the carriers of opposing social persuasions. On one side stood the party of the war effort, the Union and, with growing explicitness, the cause of Negro freedom and citizenship. On the other side stood the Democrats, a party infected by Negrophobia, eager for a negotiated peace, firmly opposed to the concept of the unified Nation, the Great Republic. *As Harper's Weekly* put it after the Democratic convention: "in surrendering to the ghost of Calhoun and the threats of South Carolina, the Chicago party, usurping the name of Democracy, surrendered the Nation, the Union, and the Government." The parties thus represented not only differing political interests, but the fundamentally opposed governmental and social ideologies of the war itself.

Reconstruction

In the enormously influential "The Chicago Platform" and "Compromise with the South" (13, 14), as well as in his lesser work during the campaign (15, 16), Nast conveyed the meaning that the war had come to have for the influential segment of Northern public opinion to which he spoke. Precisely because it touched on causes that transcended the ordinary political concerns of place and power, his art had a special impact on its audience. The potential of these drawings was speedily recognized by the Union Republican party, which distributed copies by the hundreds of thousands.

Lincoln's victory over McClellan in 1864 had for those committed to the Republican cause a significance comparable to the victories at Gettysburg or Atlanta. *Harper's Weekly* put into words the sense of what was at stake that Nast's pictures had tried to convey:

> the grandest lesson of the result is the vindication of the American system of free popular government. No system in history was ever so exposed to such a strain along the fibre as that which ours has endured in the war and the political campaign, and no other could possibly have endured it successfully. . . . Thank God and the people, we are a nation which comprehends its priceless importance to human progress and civilization. . . .

There was a triumph to be savored; and there was a lesson to be learned. The people, said *Harper*'s editor George W. Curtis,

> are conscious of the power and force of their own Government. They expect the utmost vigor in the prosecution of the war by every legitimate method, and they naturally require that the authority of the Government, which is to be established by the continuance of the war, shall not be endangered by its end.

It is not surprising that men who were passionately committed to the Union and to human freedom, and ready to see the government of the Nation continue to assert its newfound strength, took a strong line on postwar policy toward the defeated South. Radical Reconstruction is remembered chiefly as the product of dogmatic ideologues—Thaddeus Stevens, Charles Sumner—and of power-hungry Republican politicos. But it is important to recognize that the fundamental postulates of Radical Reconstruction—that unregenerate white Southerners could not readily be allowed to reassume power, that the Federal government had a special obligation to protect the political and social rights of the freedmen—had wide currency among the most influential shapers of Northern public sentiment. Curtis of *Harper's Weekly* was typical in that he had been slow to warm to the social implications of the war; typically, too, his ardor would be quick to cool. But in the fevered time around the end of the war he thought differently. Lecturing during the 1864-65 season, he told his listeners: "we are mad if the blood of the war has not anointed our eyes to see that all reconstruction is vain that leaves any question too brittle to handle. Whatever in this country, in its moral condition of peace, is too delicate to discuss is too dangerous to tolerate." Under his direction *Harper's Weekly* in the postwar years became a powerful—because so solidly entrenched—spokesman for the precepts of Republican Radicalism. The great voices of New England opinion were just as eager to dwell on the social meaning of the war. Charles Eliot Norton ringingly declared: "Having power, we have also the right—and having the right, the duty lies upon us—to impose those conditions on the Southern people which are requisite for the preservation, continuance, and progress of the moral order of that community of which they and we form parts." Even mild Emerson asserted in April of 1865: "'Tis for the best that the rebels have been pounded instead of negotiated into a peace. They must remember it." The influential Congregational magazine *The Independent* asserted in May 1865: "There is one, and only one, sure and safe policy for the immediate future, namely: *The North must remain the absolute dictator of the Republic until the spirit of the North shall become the spirit of the whole country.*"

Nast fully accepted this reading of the war's meaning. As much as anyone he helped to create Northern support that for a season made Radical Reconstruction politically viable. In 1867 he met the journalist and humorist David Ross Locke, the creator of Petroleum V. Nasby. Locke's Nasby letters purported to be the accounts of a prototypal hard-drinking, coarse, Negrophobic, office-seeking Copperhead Democrat. Lincoln was entranced by Locke's acerb humor, and Nasby after the war continued to serve the Republicans well as the buffoon-like archetype of their Democratic enemy. Nast and Locke collaborated to sustain the cause of Radical Republicanism during the Reconstruction years. As befitted satirists and caricaturists, they dwelt especially on the venality, anti-Negro brutality, and disloyalty of Democrats. At the same time they conveyed their commitment to an active government animated by elevated social purpose. Locke later said: "Government is the most important matter on this earth"; and Nast's powerful political art affirmed the principle. In 1872 there appeared a retrospective compilation of Locke's work— *The Struggles (Social, Financial and Political) of Petroleum V.*

Nasby. Nast drew illustrations for the book, and Charles Sumner, the patron saint of Radical Reconstruction, wrote its Introduction. Of the Nasby letters and Nast's cartoons Sumner said: "they were among the influences and agencies by which disloyalty in all its forms was exposed and public opinion assured on the right side." "Each letter," said Sumner, "was like a speech, or one of those songs which stir the people"—or, he might well have added, like one of Thomas Nast's cartoons.

When Andrew Johnson assumed the Presidency in April 1865 upon Lincoln's assassination, the general expectation among Republicans was that he would impose a hard and unforgiving peace settlement upon the South. As a member of the Joint Congressional Committee on the Conduct of the War, the Union Governor of bitterly divided Tennessee, and Lincoln's Vice President, he had been an outspoken hard-liner. Radical Republican leaders Benjamin Wade of Ohio and Charles Sumner of Massachusetts believed that Johnson favored Negro suffrage. After he took office the new President told a Negro regiment: "This is your country as well as anybody's country," and recommended limited Negro voting.

But Johnson ultimately chose to march to a different drummer. He quickly brought the rebel states back into full political participation in the Union. Pleading states' rights and white supremacy, he made it clear that he was ready to abandon the freedmen to their former masters.

In part this action was political. Never at the center of the Union Republican party, Johnson sought after the war to preserve his political power by an alliance with the Democrats. And then there were the limits that his personality imposed upon his social outlook. The politician and jurist David Davis, no enemy of Johnson, thought he had "qualities totally unfitting him to be the ruler of a people in the fix we are in." The President lacked executive ability; he was "obstinate, self-willed, combative, slow to act." Lincoln's rough-hewn origins had enhanced his Presidency. But Johnson seemed to fall back on the mean and crabbed components of his indecorous past. His way with words—so important a part of American political life in the nineteenth century—coarsened and shriveled as did his political ideals and purposes. What George Julian of Indiana called Johnson's "habit of bad English and incoherence of thought" was most conspicuous during his "swing around the circle"—his hapless attempt to campaign for like-thinking Congressional candidates—in 1866. James Russell Lowell icily noted of this effort: "Mr. Johnson is the first of our Presidents who had descended to the stump, and spoken to the people as if they were a mob."

Inevitably a figure so flawed caught the eye of Thomas Nast. Johnson was the first political leader to fall subject to Nast's gift for caricature. On July 30, 1866, dozens of participants in a Radical Republican constitutional convention in New Orleans (most of them Negroes) were slaughtered by the city's white police. In his powerful commentary "Amphitreatum Johnsonianum," Nast portrayed the President as a bloodthirsty Roman Emperor, his coadjutors (Secretary of State William H. Seward, Secretary of the Navy Gideon Welles) behind him (17). Johnson took on the visage of Iago as the anti-Negro and pro-Southern implications of his Reconstruction policies emerged (18). The Congressional election of 1866, which served as a national referendum on the Johnson-Conservative-Democratic and Radical Republican views of Reconstruction, whetted Nast's pencil. In September the Conservatives held a convention in Philadelphia which stressed the restored harmony of North and South, a fellowship of reconciliation ripe for the artist's ridicule (19). Equally vulnerable was Johnson's effort to assert himself as a strong President (20).

Caricature had become a major weapon in Nast's artistic arsenal. Hereafter his political commentary rarely would have the abstract quality that characterized his wartime work. Instead, he created a political world peopled by lampooned statesmen. Both his art and his influence would be the beneficiaries.

The triumph of Radical Reconstruction depended on more than the insufficiencies of the President and the ambitions of Republican politicians. Northern emotions stirred by the grinding years of war could not readily be put to rest. The memory of so much death and suffering needed the balm of a substantial assurance that the cost had been worthwhile, that the ideals fought for would be translated into reality.

Nast spoke powerfully to this theme. He had the memory of the war's human cost haunt a restless Uncle Sam (21). Bitterly he contrasted the wartime suffering of Union prisoners in notorious Andersonville and the relatively gentle treatment accorded Jefferson Davis in his confinement at Fortress Monroe (22). (A more pleasant irony lay in the fact that a Negro, Hiram Revels, occupied the Senate seat from Mississippi once held by Jefferson Davis (23).) The brutal treatment of Negroes, Unionists, and Republicans by unregenerate Southern whites kept Northern feelings high (24, 25).

44

Reconstruction

So in the postwar years there developed a Northern sense of the South as unaccepting, uncowed. Inevitably the Presidential election of 1868 reflected the deep national division over postwar policy: whether to restore the Union as it was (less the right to own slaves and to secede), or to go on to a federally enforced guarantee of Negro rights that would profoundly affect the social and political life of the South—and of the nation.

The Republicans at Chicago in May 1868 gave their Presidential nomination to the man who represented the essence of the Union cause: Ulysses S. Grant (26). The Democrats acted, in Nast's eyes, with a similar sense of the appropriate. Their candidate, Governor Horatio Seymour of New York, had been a prominent critic of the Union war effort. Now he was the candidate of a party seemingly dominated by two brutish, unregenerate elements: the urban Irish of the North and unreconstructed Southern Confederates of the stamp of Nathan B. Forrest, perpetrator of the Fort Pillow massacre of Negro Union troops (27).

Nast directed the full force of his powers of caricature at the Democratic candidate. He portrayed Seymour as Lady Macbeth, seeking vainly to rid himself of the taint of the New York City draft riots of 1863 (28). Then the artist found that Seymour's hair by a few strokes of the pencil could become the Devil's horns—and he had the characterization that served him for the rest of the campaign (29).

The parties' stands on the place of Negroes in American life summed up their differing social values. The Republicans offered freedmen the chance to lead ordinary and respectable—if separate—lives (30). Democrats sought either to woo the votes of Negroes in unseemly ways (with the assistance of Chief Justice Salmon P. Chase, still pursuing the will-o'-the-wisp of the Presidency)—or to deprive the freedmen of the vote, of life itself (31, 32).

Nast, it appeared, was to be as important a force in postwar public opinion as he had been during the war. Grant was supposed to have said after his victory in 1868: "Two things elected me: the sword of Sheridan [a reference to Federal troops in the South that ensured Negro voting] and the pencil of Nast." The artist had helped to rally popular sentiment to the cause of the Union in wartime; now he contributed in equal measure to political victory over those forces that threatened the postwar Republican hegemony. When in March 1869 Grant replaced Johnson in the Presidency, Nast might well assume that the triumph of Radical Republicanism was complete (33).

RESOLVED,—THAT IN THE FUTURE, AS IN THE PAST, WE WILL ADHERE WITH UNSWERVING FIDELITY TO THE UNION UNDER THE CONSTITUTION, AS THE ONLY SOLID FOUNDATION OF OUR STRENGTH

THE CHIC

SECURITY, AND HAPPINESS AS A PEOPLE, AND AS A FRAME-WORK OF GOVERNMENT EQUALLY CONDUCIVE TO THE WELFARE AND PROSPERITY OF ALL THE STATES, BOTH NORTHERN AND SOUTHERN.

RESOLVED,—THAT THIS CONVENTION DOES EXPLICITLY DECLARE, AS THE SENSE OF THE AMERICAN PEOPLE, THAT, AFTER FOUR YEARS OF FAILURE TO RESTORE THE UNION, B DURING WHICH, UNDER THE PRETENSE OF A MILITARY NECESSI POWER HIGHER THAN OF A WAR, THE CONSTITUTION

THE CONSTITUTION ITSELF HAS BEEN DISREGARDED IN EVERY PART, AND PUBLIC LIBERTY AND PRIVATE RIGHT

ALIKE TRODDEN DOWN, AND THE MATERIAL PROSPERITY OF THE COUNTRY ESSENTIALLY IMPAIRED, JUSTICE, HUMANITY, LIBERTY,

GEORGE B. McCLELLAN

AND THE PUBLIC WELFARE, DEMAND THAT IMMEDIATE EFFORTS BE MADE FOR A CESSATION OF HOSTILITIES WITH A VIEW TO AN ULTIMATE CONVENTION OF ALL THE STATES,

CONVENTION OF ALL THE STATES

OR OTHER PEACABLE MEANS TO THE END THAT AT THE EARLIEST PRACTICABLE MOMENT PEACE MAY BE RESTORED ON THE BASIS OF THE FEDERAL UNION OF THE STATES.

MEETING AT UNION SQUARE FOR PRESIDENT JEFF. DAVIS 1868.

[13]

O PLATFORM.

October 15, 1864

COMPROMISE WITH THE SOUTH.

Dedicated to the Chicago Convention.

September 3, 1864

[14]

TO
MY COUNTRY
FOR WHICH I HAVE FOUGHT AND DIED.

A
CURSE UPON
YOU, FOR MAKING ME APPEAR DISLOYAL

KILLED
IN THE
WAR
FOR THE
UNION.

November 12, 1864

How the Copperheads Obtain Their Votes.

[15]

ELECTION-DAY,
8TH NOVEMBER.
1864.

NO COMPROMISE.

DOWN WITH SLAVERY.

DOWN WITH THE REBELS.

THE ELECTION OF THE UNION CANDIDATES WILL BRING PEACE.

THE VICTORY AT THE
BALLOT-BOX WILL BE IN VINDICATION OF THIS UNION AND OF OUR AUTHORITY

CITIZENS VOTING.

THE VETERAN'S VOTE.

SOLDIERS
MAILING THEIR VOTES

[17]

March 30, 1867

Amphitheatrum Johnsonianum—Massacre of the Innocents
At New Orleans, July 30, 1866.

ANDREW JOHNSON'S RECONSTRUCTION.

TREASON IS A CRIME AND MUST BE MADE ODIOUS, AND TRAITORS MUST BE PUNISHED.

RIOTS.

NEW ORLEANS.

RADICAL(S)
SOUTHERN RIGHTS

LINCOLN CHAPEL

MEMPHIS.

WHAT THEY WERE.

AUCTION SALE

VETOES.

TO
UNION
MEN

JOHNSON. VETOES.

FREEDMEN'S BUREAU
No. 1

CIVIL RIGHTS BILL
No. 2

AMENDMENT TO THE U.S.
CONSTITUTION OBJECT TO

Dr. P. B. RANDOLPH, A COLORED MAN,
HAD DINNER AND A GRATEFUL
CLASS OF WINE AT THE WHITE
HOUSE.

SEE N.Y. TIMES

I AM ONE
OF YOUR
BEST
FRIENDS.

JOHNSON'S
PLANTATION

LOVE THINE
ENEMIES

I AM YOUR
MOSES

PARDON TO REBELS

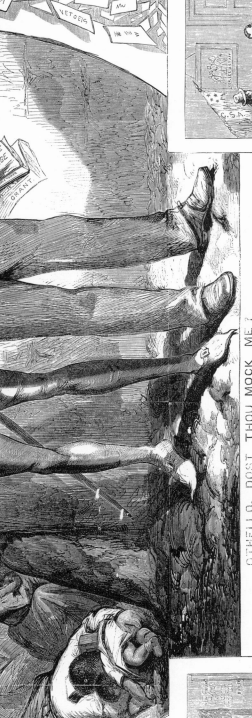

OTHELLO. DOST THOU MOCK ME?

IAGO. I MOCK YOU! NO, BY HEAVEN:
WOULD YOU WOULD BEAR YOUR FORTUNES LIKE A MAN.

SHAKSPEARE.

HOW AND IT WORKS.

Th. Nast.

1862.

1866.

Iago. The Moor is of a free and open nature,
That thinks men honest that but seem to be so;
And will as tenderly be led by the nose,
As asses......
Make the Moor thank me, love me, and reward me.
For making him egregiously an ass,
And practising upon his peace and quiet
Even to madness. 'Tis here, but yet confus'd......
Knavery's plain face is never seen, till us'd......
Though I do hate him as I do hell-pains,
Yet, for necessity of present life,
I must show out a flag and sign of love;
Which is indeed but sign......
Then devils will their blackest sins put on,
They do suggest at first with heavenly shows,
As I do now......
I humbly do beseech you of your pardon,
For too much loving you.
I hope, you will consider, what is spoke
Comes from my love;—But, I do see you are mov'd:—
I am to pray you, not to strain my speech
To grosser issues, nor to larger reach
Than to suspicion.

Are you a man? have you a soul, or sense?—
God be wi' you; take mine office.—O wretched fool,
That liv'st to make thine honesty a vice!—
O monstrous world! Take note, take note, O world!
To be direct and honest, is not safe.—
I thank you for this profit, and from hence,
I'll love no friend, since love breeds such offence......

My medicine, work!

Work on,

Othello.

"I have been accused of being inimical to the true
interests of the colored people; but this is not true. I
am one of their best friends; and time, which tries and
tests all, will demonstrate the fact......I once said I
would be the Moses of your people, and lead them on to
liberty—liberty they now have......I have been blamed
for vetoing the Freedmen's Bureau Bill, and have done it
because I was their enemy. This is not true......The
ordinary course of judicial proceedings is no longer inter-
rupted. The courts, both State and Federal, are in full,
complete, and successful operation, and through them
every person, regardless of race and color, is entitled to
and can be heard. The protection granted to the white
citizen is already conferred by law upon the freedman.
......It can not be expected that men who have for four
years been made familiar with the blood and carnage of
war, who have suffered the loss of property, and in so
many instances reduced from affluence to poverty, can at
once assume the calm demeanor and action of those citizens of the country whose worldly possessions have not
been destroyed, and whose political hopes have not been
blasted, and the worst view of this subject affords no par-
allel in violence to similar outrages that have followed all
civil commotions, always less in magnitude than ours.
But I do not believe that this to-be-regretted state of
things will last long."—ANDREW JOHNSON.

September 1, 1866

[18]

THE SPIRIT OF CONCORD AND BROTHERLY AFFECTION.

CONVENTION

EVERY EYE WAS SUFFUSED WITH TEARS ON BEHOLDING THE SCENE.

TEARS OF JOY AND GRATITUDE.

THE
EVENT FILLING THE EYES OF THOUSANDS WITH TEARS OF JOY,

FIRST GUN.

FIRST BLOOD.

THE TEARFUL CONVENTION

MASSACHUSETTS AND SOUTH CAROLINA COMING ARM IN ARM INTO THE CONVENTION.

Th. Nast.

INTELLECT.

WISDOM.

"I COULD NOT FINISH READING THE DISPATCH FOR MY OWN FEELINGS OVERCAME ME."

PATRIOTIC SENTIMENT.

UNBROKEN HARMONY.

WHY HE CANNOT SLEEP.

[21]

July 7, 1866

THE CONTRAST OF SUFFERING. ANDERSONVILLE & FORTRESS MONROE.

Th. Nast.

TREASON MUST BE MADE ODIOUS.

June 30, 1866

"TIME WORKS WONDERS."

IAGO. (JEFF DAVIS.) "FOR THAT I DO SUSPECT THE LUSTY MOOR
HATH LEAP'D INTO MY SEAT : THE THOUGHT WHEREOF
DOTH LIKE A POISONOUS MINERAL GNAW MY INWARDS." — OTHELLO.

[23]

April 9, 1870

TIMELY WARNING,

TO UNION MEN.

THE NEW-ORLEANS

CONVENTION   OR   MASSACRE.

WHICH IS THE MORE ILLEGAL.

September 8, 1866

TENNESSEE.

THE MURDER OF SENATOR CASE.

VIRGINIA.

DRIVING THEM OFF THE PLANTATIONS WITHOUT WAGES AND SHOOTING THEM

IF HE IS A SOUTHERN GENTLEMAN,

VERDICT, "A GOOD JOKE ON A NIGGER".

SOUTH CAROLINA.

THREE U.S. SOLDIERS MURDERED.

TWENTYTWO NEGRO PRISONERS BURNED TO DEATH.

And the President's V

Journal's special correspondence says that a mob, composed of
Quantrell's guerrillas, broke open Mr. Carey's house at Parkesv
and hung Mr. Carey. He had been tried for stealing a horse to
rebe's at the batt'e of Perrysville.

CHARLESTON, SOUTH CAROLINA.—Three soldiers of the army
States were murdered in October, 1865, in South Carolina, under c
peculiar cruelty, and several persons were arrested, tried, and c
military commission for said murder. Said persons, so condemn
quently reprieved and transferred to Fort Delaware, from which t
by writ of habeas corpus and set free.

Jan., 1867.—" The jail at Kingstree, South Carolina, has been de
and 22 colored prisoners smothered or burned to death, while the
oner was permitted to escape."—MAJOR-GENERAL J. C. ROBINSO

BELL COUNTY, TEXAS.—On the night of December 3 a mob
entered the jail, murdered old Mr. Lindley, his son, and another in
who was an entire stranger to the Lindleys......GRAYSON COUNTY
have been most brutally murdered within the last few days.

SAVANNAH, GEORGIA.—The police, however, arrested several
they treated in the most brutal and barbarous manner—beating ther
so severely as to cause the blood to flow profusely. No attempt
arrest any of the white men, although they were the parties who i
controlled the strike from beginning to end.

" Driving them off plantations without wages, or, as has bee
cases, shooting them ; a gentleman who commits a homicide of tha
gentlemen friends together—and they are nearly all magistrates—
ine and discharge him."—GENERAL SCHOFIELD, *Department of*

" My own opinion is that the trial of a white man for the murde
in Texas would be a farce, and in making the statement I make
comrels me, and for no other rea-on."—GENERAL SHERIDAN.

" You could not find a jury in South Carolina that would convic
ing a Union soldier, no matter what the testimony."—GENERAL S

" Homicides of Union men, soldiers, and freedmen, are on the in
ERAL THOMAS J. WOOD.

" If a freedman is murdered by men who had been in the rebelli
sible to get the criminal arrested even ; and if he is arrested, he i
leased on very low bail."—GENERAL BAIRD.

" I do not believe there is much chance of convicting a resid
Georgia for murder if the victim is a Union man or a negro."—G

SOUTHE

GEORGIA.

THE POLICE AND THE FREEDMEN.

KENTUCKY.

THE HANGING OF Mr. CAREY.

IF HE IS A UNION MAN OR A FREEDMAN.

'VERDICT ", HANG THE D— YANKEE AND NIGGER".

TEXAS

THE LINDLEY MURDER.

WHOLESALE MURDER OF FREEDMEN.

...tary Government Bill.

...at there exists in those States no legal Governments, and no ade-
...n for life or property, and asserts the necessity of enforcing peace
... within their limits.....They are organized like the other States
...nd like them they make, administer, and execute the laws which
...omestic affairs......The provisions which these Governments have
...eservation of order, the suppression of crime, and the redress of
... are in substance and principle the same as those which prevail in
...States and in other civilized countries .....It is undoubtedly true
... have been much increased and exaggerated, North and South, by
...g influences of civil war, and by the rancorous passions which the
...gendered.....The military rule which it establishes is plainly to
...any purpose of order, or for the prevention of crime, but solely as
...rcing the people into the adoption of principles and measures to
...own that they are opposed, and upon which they have an undenia-
...rcise their own judgment.....The power thus given to the com-
...over all the people of each district is that of an absolute monarch.
...ound by no State law, and there being no other law to regulate the
... make a criminal code of his own, and he can make it as bloody as
... history, or he can reserve the privilege of acting upon the impulse
...passions in each case that arises ....Instead of *mitigating* the
...sponsibility of making it more cruel and unjust......Can it be ex-
...itary officers will understand or follow a rule expressed in language
...ical, and not pertaining in the least degree to their profession? If
...officer may define cruelty according to his own temper, and if not
...make it usual. Corporal punishment—the gag, the ball and chain,
...almost insupportable forms of torture invented for military punish-
...n the range of choice......It is plain that the authority here given
... officer amounts to absolute despotism......It reduces the whole
...he ten States, all persons of every color, sex, and condition, and ev-
...hin their limits, to the most abject and degrading slavery......It
...ly the citizens of the United States which are within the Union, but
... human being who comes or is brought under our jurisdiction......
...te comprised in the five military districts life, liberty, and property
...State laws and Federal laws, and the national Constitution is every
...and every where obeyed. The Courts, State and Federal, are open
...exercise of their proper authority. What, then, is the ground on
...proceeds?......We are providing now for a time of profound peace,
...not an armed soldier within our borders except those who are in the
...Government..... The Constitution declares that no person shall be
...e, liberty, or property without due process of law .....The evils
...om the unsettled state of our Government will be acknowledged by
...ox.

March 23, 1867

June 6, 1868

Chicago, May 21, 1868.

September 5, 1868

"This Is a White Man's Government."

"We regard the Reconstruction Acts (so called) of Congress as usurpations, and unconstitutional, revolutionary, and void."—*Democratic Platform.*

[28]   September 19, 1868

Time, midnight.—*Scene*, New York City Hall.
LADY *******. "Out, damned spot! out, I say! . . . Here's the smell of the blood
still: all the perfumes of Democracy will not sweeten this little hand. Oh! oh! oh!"

"Let us have Peace."—*Republican Candidate for President.*

"What the Confederacy fought for would be won by the Election of Seymour and Blair."—*Vance.*

"Let the President disperse the Carpet-Bag State Government."—*Democratic Candidate for Vice-President.*

September 19, 1868

"Lead Us Not Into Temptation."

[29]

September 26, 1868

"But—"

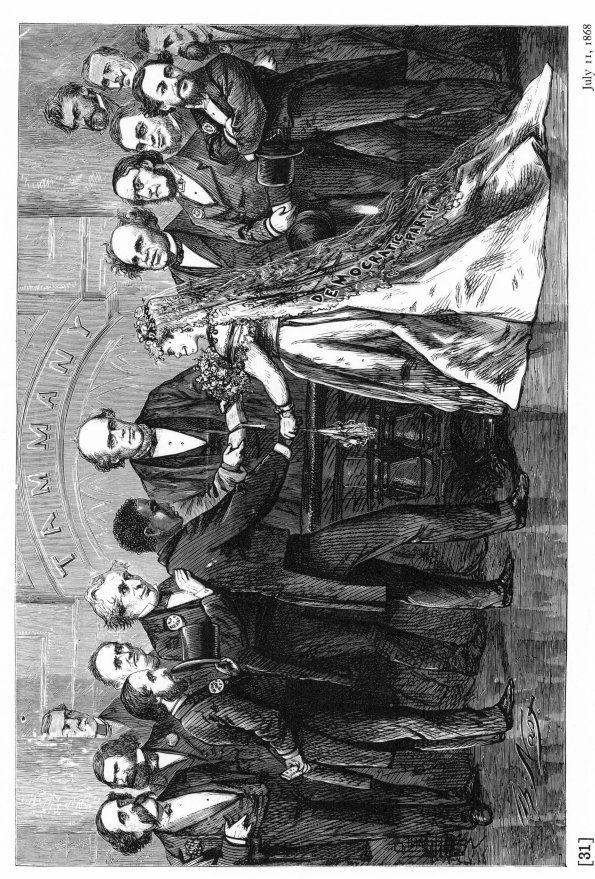

"Would you Marry Your Daughter to a Nigger?"

REV. DR. CHASE (*to the Bride*). "Do you promise to love, honor, and obey—?"
THE BRIDE. "*Don't I?*"

[31]

October 3, 1868

The Modern Samson.

[32]

[33]

"Liberty! Freedom! Tyranny is dead!
Run hence, proclaim, cry it about the streets."

"Some to the common pulpits, and cry out
LIBERTY, FREEDOM, AND ENFRANCHISEMENT!"

March 13, 1869

The Political Death of the Bogus Caesar.

IV
Liberal Republicanism

The political passions of the Civil War and Reconstruction faded with the passing of years. Men and interests changed; American public life began to reflect the compelling pull of new issues. But Thomas Nast's prime political loyalties—to Grant, to the Republican party, to the causes and ideals of the war era—did not readily recede. The parties remained for him the repositories of deeply opposed social values. Such a view of American politics, whatever its objective reality, served to sustain the passionate commitments of the war era in less clear-cut and decisive times. One has the sense that this was the case for many of Nast's generation. If so, it explains much of the ardent partisan feeling that kept the parties something more than technical devices for the attainment of political power.

Nast, then, approached the 1872 Presidential election campaign with an undiminished partisanship. The Republican party remained the instrument of Union, of progress and liberalism, of humanity; the Democrats remained the voice of secession, of reaction, of Negrophobia and violence (34).

But many others who were actively engaged in political life did not share his unshaken commitment to Republican solidarity. The façade of party unity sustained by the confrontation with Andrew Johnson and the Democrats began to crack almost as soon as Grant took office in 1869. Republican dissidence quickly took on an organized political form. In 1872 it emerged as the national Liberal Republican movement, ready to run a Presidential candidate against the regular party nominee.

Liberal Republicanism did not have an elaborate party machinery, nor was it the political voice of a broad, popular sentiment. At base it was a set of policy positions—and a set of men. Liberal Republicans readily committed themselves to the legislative achievements of the Reconstruction era—to the thirteenth, fourteenth and fifteenth Amendments and to "the equality of all men before the law." But they were anxious to see existing political disabilities on Confederate leaders removed and Federal troops withdrawn from the South. "Local self-government," their 1872 platform argued, "will guard the rights of all citizens more securely than any centralized power." That the results of these policies would be Democratic control of the South—and white control of Southern Negroes—did not disturb them. Their first desire was to escape from the tormenting issues—and political commitments—of the war and Reconstruction years.

At the same time, Liberal Republicans sought to focus national attention on a new set of public concerns. One of these was government corruption and the need for a civil service system. Another was the level of tariff protection, and the desirability of lower rates. They wanted also the rapid resumption of specie payments on greenbacks to sustain the public credit, and the end of government land grants to railroads and other private corporations.

Liberal Republicanism co-existed in time and spirit with the so-called "New Departure" movement within the Democratic party. Democrats, too, sought to escape from the issues of the Civil War decade by accepting (at least in principle) the Reconstruction amendments and dwelling instead on the tariff, civil service reform, and corporate power. The national Democratic party in 1872 adopted both the platform and the candidate of the Liberal Republicans.

But to stress the shared views of Democrats and Liberal Republicans raises certain problems. The Liberal Republican movement included men who had been important and committed figures in the politics of anti-slavery and of Radical Reconstruction: Senators Charles Sumner of Massachusetts, Carl Schurz of Missouri, and Lyman Trumbull of Illinois; editors Horace Greeley of the *New York Tribune*, Samuel Bowles of the *Springfield Republican*, and Horace White of the *Chicago Tribune*. Now they were ready to drop the great causes of the recent past, to abandon Southern Negroes to the notably untender mercies of their white neighbors, to leave the party of the Union. Why were they ready to do these things? And why did Thomas Nast—surely their peer in his commitment to a politics of morality, of elevated social purpose—refuse to join them? Why did he, instead, subject the Liberal Republican leaders to a ridicule and condemnation as keen, as deeply felt as his treatment of Andrew Johnson and the Democrats?

Complex considerations of personal ambition and ideological leaning determined individual political paths in 1872. But fundamentally the Liberal Republican movement attracted men for whom the tone, the leadership—one might say the culture—of the Republican party had become intolerable. Sumner, Schurz, and Trumbull—pioneers in the establishment of the party—felt now that it had come into the hands of gross and impure men: social and political *arrivistes*. Grant himself —taciturn, redolent of cigars and whiskey—was the great symbol of this decline. No less offensive was the group of party leaders whose company and counsel Grant clearly preferred: Oliver Morton of Indiana, Zachariah Chandler of Michigan, Roscoe Conkling of New York, the ineffable Benjamin F. Butler of Massachusetts. Most of these men (not least Grant himself) had come to their Republicanism much later than Sumner, Schurz, or Trumbull; and they had been Democrats, not Whigs, to begin with. Theirs was the Republican party of the war and Reconstruction, of success and power, of organization and force; not the party of its purer, leaner early days.

George W. Julian of Indiana, a Republican founding father and leader of the Liberal Republican movement, feelingly described the transformation. Republicanism at first "was not a party at all. It was merely a political combination. Its action was not inspired by a creed, but an *object*"—the end of slavery and the perpetuation of the Union. But by the very fact of their postwar existence the Republicans became "a faction, led by base men, and held together by artful appeals to the memories of common struggles." The new Republican leaders "were not only in favor of perpetuating the organization, but they treat it as an institution."

Liberal Republicanism was the cause of those who were politically displaced by this change. It is significant that newspaper editors played an especially important role in the movement. Journalists were men of political power in the antislavery and war years. Those were times when political combinations—the prewar Republican party, the wartime Union coalition—were held together by causes more than by organization. Horace Greeley's *Tribune* for a generation was a force of the first consequence in American public life. But now the power of party organization, and the emotive appeal of party loyalty, threatened the hegemony of the editors. The man of the organization had become more important than the man of the word.

Finally, men of genteel breeeding, who had high hopes for their political influence in postwar America, were drawn to the Liberal Republican cause. Henry Adams, his brother Charles Francis Adams, and the economist David Ames Wells are examples of the type. They, too, were frustrated by postwar American political life: perennially tempted by what it offered, perennially unsatisfied by what it gave.

But not all Republicans of ideals and sensitivity suffered this disillusionment. Thomas Nast in the postwar years did not experience the loss of power and influence that afflicted Greeley or Sumner. Quite the contrary: he became an ever more respected—and feared—figure in a political environment where the ability to lampoon the opposition, to stir the emotions of the party faithful, was an important talent. Nast visited Washington in early 1872, and had the heady pleasure of being the lion of the season. He told his wife of a party given "for the Great men of Washington to meet me, and I can tell you they came, with a vengens [*sic*]. . . . the power I have is *terrible*."

He had, too, an emotional relationship to the Republican party different from that of the Liberal Republicans. His commitment to the party was a product of the war. Antislavery and the sanctity of the Union never existed for him as causes outside of the context of the party, as it did for many of the Republican pioneers. In consequence, the party as an institution remained too tightly bound up with his social beliefs for him readily to abandon it.

Confident and unshaken in his Republicanism, Nast reacted strongly to the criticism levelled against the Grant administration by Sumner, Schurz, Trumbull, and others. He savagely caricatured these Senators for their presumption in attacking the hero of the age (35, 36, 37, 38, 39).

George W. Curtis, the political editor of *Harper's Weekly*, was close to the Liberal Republicans personally and in spirit. He objected to the violence of Nast's commentary, accusing the artist of "lack of moral perception." For some months in 1872 there was a coolness between the two men. "There is a very great pressure against me, about my making fun against Sumner Schurz etc.," Nast told his wife, "but

I hear that the Harpers will stick by me, no matter what will happen, and if things come to the worst Curtis will have to go." They differed profoundly in their approach to political commentary: Curtis the man of letters (and of frustrated political ambitions), of New England Brahmin culture; Nast the slightly educated young man (he was only 32 in 1872), rough-and-tumble in his talent and his politics. The artist said of Curtis and himself: "When he attacks a man with his pen it seems as if he were apologizing for the act. I try to hit the enemy between the eyes and knock him down."

The gulf between them was social too. Nast took note of Curtis's displeasure over the attendance of so many "gentlemen" at a party in the artist's honor. He said of Secretary of State Hamilton Fish: "he is a gentleman but does not like Mr. Curtis very much"—a conjunction unusual enough to note.

Supported by publisher Fletcher Harper, Nast subjected the Liberal Republican movement to a sustained and coruscating attack. One object of his scorn was the Cincinnati convention at which the Liberal Republicans came to the unlikely choice of Horace Greeley as their Presidential candidate (40, 41). The Democrats' ready acceptance of both Greeley and the Liberal Republican platform confirmed Nast's judgment that here was a betrayal of the great cause of the war. He commented with appropriate irony on the fact that Greeley, for decades the voice of antislavery and high tariff Republicanism, now was the candidate of the Negrophobic, Tammany-dominated, secession-minded Democracy (42, 43, 44, 45).

Through the months of the 1872 campaign Nast developed his view of Greeley as the epitome of muddled vagary. (He had no photograph of B. Gratz Brown of Missouri, Greeley's running mate, and so hit on the splendidly anonymous symbol of the slip of paper, inscribed with Brown's name, attached to the Greeley coattail.) He dwelt especially on the ironic potential of Greeley's call to the Democrats at their Baltimore convention to "clasp hands over the bloody chasm." Dozens of richly caricatured Democratic and Liberal Republican leaders crowded his drawings, a sinister *dramatis personae* of the Greeley campaign (46, 47, 48, 49, 50, 51, 52).

Greeley suffered overwhelming defeat in the fall election. Democratic voters never warmed to a candidacy in so many ways offensive to their party sensibilities. And the mass of Republicans remained loyal to a view of their party—and of the Greeley candidacy—close to that of Nast. Mark Twain told him: "Nast, you more than any other man have won a prodigious victory for Grant—I mean, rather, for Civilization and Progress. Those pictures were simply marvelous." The artist celebrated the tidal wave of public repudiation of the Liberal Republican-Democratic venture, and the triumph of Grant and the party of Liberty and Union (53, 54).

But Nast's political universe—and his artistic power—never again would be so secure. For all their personal frustrations, Liberal Republicans accurately described the course of Republican politics—indeed, of American politics at large. And as the political dialogue moved from the issues of the war years, the loyalty even of so ardent a partisan as Thomas Nast ultimately would be strained beyond its limits.

REPUBLICAN PRINCIPLES

DEMOCRATIC PRINCIPLES.

May 6, 1871

[34]

June 15, 1872

"Played Out!"

June 22, 1872

The Last Shot of the Honorable Senator from Massachusetts.—
He Pulled the Long-Bow Once Too Often.

March 16, 1872

[37]

The "Liberal" Conspirators (Who, You All Know, Are Honorable Men).

"O, let us have him; for his silver hair
Will purchase us a good opinion,
And buy men's voices to commend our deeds:

It shall be said, his judgment rul'd our hands;
Our youths, and wildness, shall no whit appear,
But all be buried in his gravity."—*Julius Caesar*.

April 13, 1872

The Republic Is Not Ungrateful.

"It is not what is *charged* but what is *proved* that damages the party defendant. Any one may be accused of the most heinous offenses; the Saviour of mankind was not only arraigned but convicted; but what of it? Facts alone are decisive."—*New York Tribune*, March 13, 1872.

"*THE TREE IS KNOWN BY HIS FRUIT.*"

[Copied from one of Mr. Greeley's Missouri Organs.]

Lexington Caucasian.

STATE SOVEREIGNTY!

WHITE SUPREMACY!

—AND—

REPUDIATION!

THIS IS LIBERTY!

Our Motto.

Never Despair of the Republic!

Our Platform.

The Constitution of 1860, and the Rights of the States!

Our Doctrines.

This is a White Man's Government, made by White Men, for White Men, and their Posterity, Forever!

DOWN WITH the FIFTEENTH BEDAMNEDMENT!

Total Repudiation of the Monstrous Yankee War Debt!—That Accursed, Unconstitutional Burden, accumulated by an Unconstitutional Mob styling itself a Congress, in the prosecution of an Unconstitutional Crusade, for the Accomplishment of an Unconstitutional and Horrid Purpose!

DOWN WITH BOND-HOLDERS AND TAXATION!

Subordination of the Military to the Civil Authorities.

DOWN WITH THE SATRAPS!

Equal Taxation and the Rightful Representation of all the States, or

ANOTHER REBELLION!

Revolution must be met by Counter Revolution! —Force by Force!—Violence by Violence! —And Usurpation should be Overthrown, if needs be, by the Bayonet!

DOWN WITH TEST OATHS and REGISTRATIONS!

VIVE LA REPUBLIQUE!

FOR PRESIDENT,

HORACE GREELEY,
OF NEW YORK.

FOR VICE PRESIDENT,

B. GRATZ BROWN,
OF MISSOURI.

U.S. GRANT

ARBITRATION 1872

SHERMAN
SHERIDAN
THOMAS
FARRAGUT
UNION AND
SOLDIERS AND
SAILORS

LIBERTY
AMNESTY
EQUAL RIGHTS

VICTORY

VICKSBURG
RICHMOND
GETTYSBURG
FORT DONELSON

STANTON
GULF &c.
SUMNER
H WILSON

EMANCIPATION
CONSTITUTION

LINCOLN

THE REPUBLICAN COLUMN.

UNION

July 27, 1872

"Any Thing for Revenge!"—à la Commune.

April 20, 1872

Will Robinson Crusoe (Sumner) Forsake His Man Friday?
The Boat's Crew That Is Going Over.

"Great Expectations."

"A (Mud) Mountain was once greatly agitated. Loud Groans and Noises were heard; and crowds of People came from all Parts to see what was the Matter. After long expectation and many wise conjectures from the by-standers, out popped a—Mouse!"

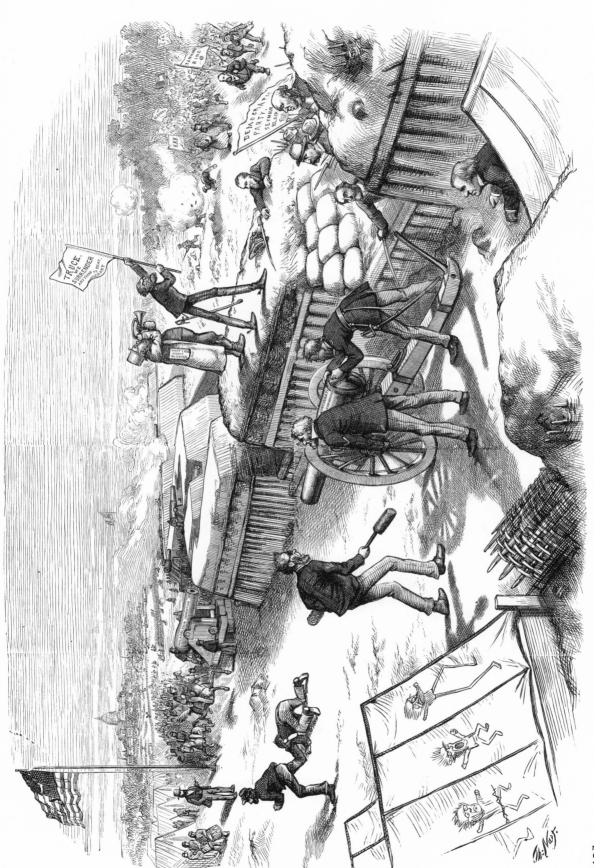

May 11, 1872

A "Liberal" Surrender—"Any Thing To Beat Grant."

[42]

July 27, 1872

The Death-Bed Marriage.

The daughter of Democracy has at last married a "nigger!" (a Radical Black Republican)—July 10, 1872.

[43]

"Old Honesty."

"If he does still think that all the vilest classes ('*blacklegs, pugilists, keepers of dens, criminals, shoulder-bitters, rowdies, burglars,*' etc., etc.), all the scum and dregs of the community, are drawn to the Democratic party by '*a sympathetic chord,*' he disgraces himself in asking for Democratic suffrages."—*New York World*, June 6, 1872.

August 3, 1872

Diogenes Has Found the Honest Man.—
(Which Is Diogenes, and Which Is the Honest Man?)

"As soon as the news that GREELEY and BROWN had been nominated was received, bunting was unfurled from every flag-staff on the *City Hall*. In the *City Hall Park* was displayed a large banner, bearing the inscription: TAMMANY RESPONDS TO THE NOMINATIONS OF THE NATIONAL CONVENTION AT BALTIMORE."—*New York Tribune*, July 11, 1872.

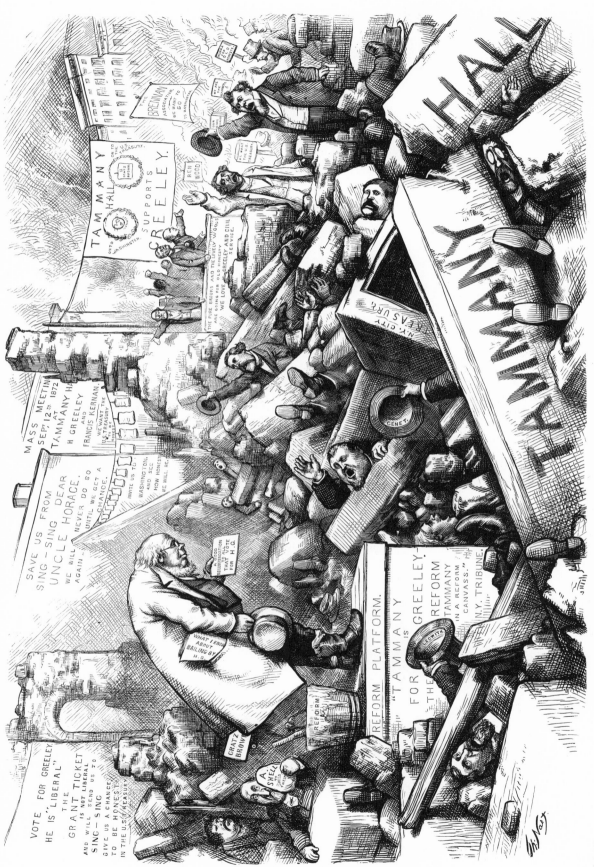

October 5, 1872

"Old Honesty" Among the Ruins of Tammany.

[46]

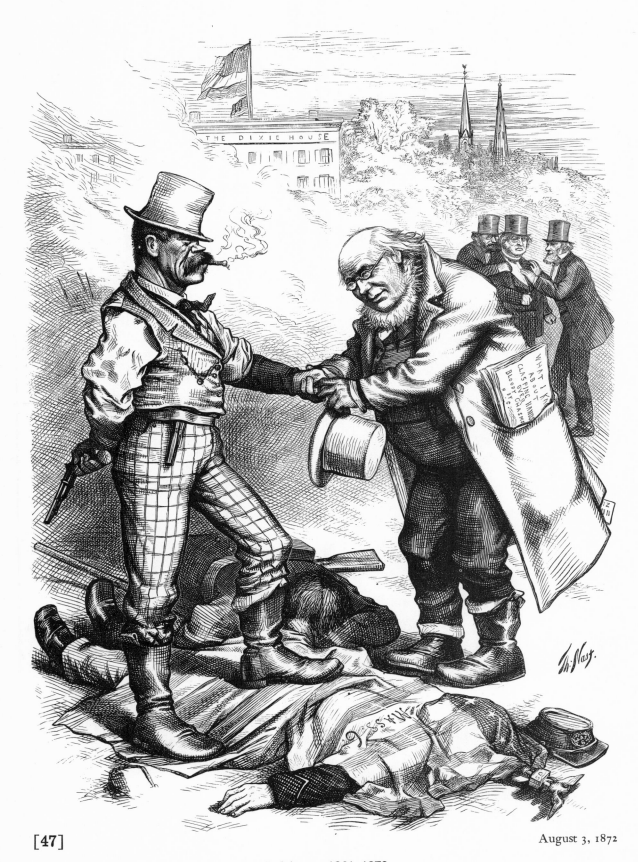

August 3, 1872

Baltimore 1861–1872.

"Let Us Clasp Hands over the Bloody Chasm."

September 21, 1872

"Let Us Clasp Hands over the Bloody Chasm."—Horace Greeley.

[48]

August 24, 1872

It Is Only a Truce To Regain Power ("Playing Possum").

H. G. "Clasp hands over the bloody chasm."
C. S. "Freely accept the hand that is offered, and reach forth thine own in friendly grasp."

[49]

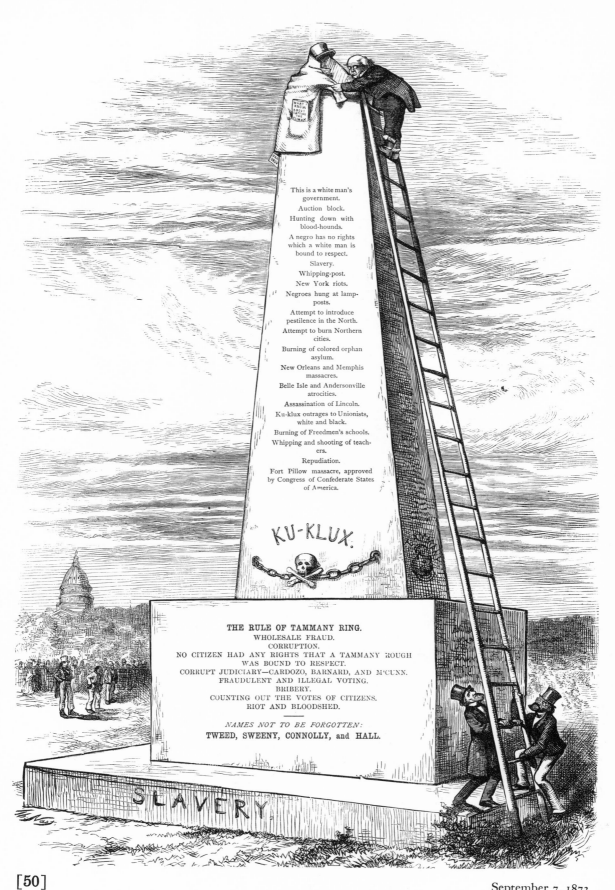

This is a white man's
government.

Auction block.

Hunting down with
blood-hounds.

A negro has no rights
which a white man is
bound to respect.

Slavery.

Whipping-post.

New York riots.

Negroes hung at lamp-
posts.

Attempt to introduce
pestilence in the North.

Attempt to burn Northern
cities.

Burning of colored orphan
asylum.

New Orleans and Memphis
massacres.

Belle Isle and Andersonville
atrocities.

Assassination of Lincoln.

Ku-klux outrages to Unionists,
white and black.

Burning of Freedmen's schools.

Whipping and shooting of teachers.

Repudiation.

Fort Pillow massacre, approved
by Congress of Confederate States
of America.

KU-KLUX.

THE RULE OF TAMMANY RING.
WHOLESALE FRAUD.
CORRUPTION.
NO CITIZEN HAD ANY RIGHTS THAT A TAMMANY ROUGH
WAS BOUND TO RESPECT.
CORRUPT JUDICIARY—CARDOZO, BARNARD, AND M'CUNN.
FRAUDULENT AND ILLEGAL VOTING.
BRIBERY.
COUNTING OUT THE VOTES OF CITIZENS.
RIOT AND BLOODSHED.

NAMES NOT TO BE FORGOTTEN:
TWEED, SWEENY, CONNOLLY, and HALL.

SLAVERY

[50]

September 7, 1872

The Whited Sepulchre.

Covering the monument of infamy with his white hat and coat.

August 17, 1872

"Satan, Don't Get Thee Behind Me!"—Any Thing To Get Possession.

November 9, 1872

"The Pirates," under False Colors.—
Can They Capture the Ship of State?

[53]

October 26, 1872

That "Tidal Wave."—"We Are on the Home Stretch!"

Clasping Hands over the Bloodless (Sar)c(h)asm.

V

The Radical Nation

Thomas Nast's Radical Republicanism—forged in the war, tempered by storms of party controversy—was more than a political stance. It rested on a set of social values that induced him to comment on a wide range of American public issues.

Negro civil rights—particularly the right to vote—was the touchstone cause of postwar Radical Republicanism. This was the issue on which Republican-Democratic political conflict most often focused. It might seem that party expediency—the lure of Negro votes in the South and the lower North—sufficiently explains the Republican commitment. But to call for Negro suffrage and other civil rights entailed political danger as well. Negroes suffered under a heavy—and popular—burden of civil disability in most Northern states. Time and again white voters in the North made it clear that while they opposed secession and slavery, they had no desire to see Negroes enjoy the blessings of equal citizenship.

Reasons deeper than political exigency explain the adherence of so many Republican politicians, journalists, and intellectuals to the cause of Negro civil equality. Men whose public lives had been devoted to the struggle against slavery and the defense of the Union were reluctant to accept a political environment where nothing divided the parties but a lust for office. To champion the cause of the freedmen was to perpetuate the moral fervor of the war years. So at a time when racist assumptions had an important—and growing—place in intellectual circles throughout the Western world, and an overt Negrophobia prevailed among white Americans, Republican spokesmen gave lip service—and more—to the idea of the Nation as a congeries of equals.

Their effort was not limited to the Radical Reconstruction governments of the Southern states. Republican organizations in the North set out to eliminate the restrictions on Negro voting and other civil rights that encrusted state constitutions and statute books. Typical was the Minnesota platform of 1865: "The measure of a man's political rights should be neither his religion, his birthplace, his race, his color, nor any merely physical characteristics." (Typically, too, the people of the state in 1867 rejected Negro suffrage.) Michigan's Republicans declared in 1866: "we scout and scorn . . . that political blasphemy which says, 'This is the white man's Government. It is God's Government made for man!" The New York party, in a state where Irish Negrophobia was a political force of some consequence, was even more orotund:

> . . . the nation is pledged to the world, to humanity, and most of all, to the freedmen, that in all lawful ways the liberty and civil rights of every human being subject to the Government of the United States shall be protected and enforced, regardless of race, color, or condition, against every wrongful opposing law, ordinance, regulation, custom, or prejudice. . . .

Legislation approached (if it did not match) this rhetoric. Massachusetts passed the first state civil rights act a month after Appomattox; Pennsylvania followed suit in 1867, New York and Kansas in 1874. Others repealed laws that restricted the movement and legal rights of Negroes.

Major national legislation defined and reinforced the civil rights implicit in emancipation. The Civil Rights Act of April 1866 gave the freedmen national citizenship and Federal protection against state discrimination. The Fifteenth Amendment in 1870 authorized Congress to guarantee Negro voting everywhere. The Civil Rights Act of March 1875 was the last great statement of Radical Republican racial policy. Holding that the object of legislation was "to enact great principles into law," the bill declared it to be "the duty of government in its dealings with the people to mete out equal and exact justice to all," and guaranteed the right to "full and equal enjoyment of the accommodations, advantages, facilities, and privileges of inns, public conveyances on land or water, theaters, and other places of public amusement."

Of course both the spirit and the letter of this legislation were quickly, universally betrayed. Custom stripped it of much meaning from the first; and the courts soon pruned its legal force. Negroes were relegated to the status of a debased caste for almost a century to come. It is difficult to recover, through the pall of what followed, the spirit of the commitment to universal civil rights in the post-Civil War years. But the mood that underlay this legislation appears with force and clarity in the work of Thomas Nast.

Nast as a political creature had a special stake in Negro voting (55). But he looked on the mistreatment of Southern Negroes with an indignation that rested on more than party considerations. "Patience on a Monument" (56) summed up his sense of the tragic experience of the freedmen during the war and postwar years. He attacked the determination of the white South to preserve the social if not the legal structure of slavery (57), and commented bitterly on the rise of organized violence by the Ku Klux Klan and the White Leagues of the 1870's (58, 59, 60). He welcomed the Civil Rights Act of 1875 as the proper final benefice of the nation to its Negro citizens, and ridiculed those who reacted to equal rights with hypocrisy or fear (61, 62, 63).

Nast's sensitivity to the rights of minority Americans extended to others besides the embattled freedmen. His triumphant Republic was a nation of diverse peoples, welded together by self-government and universal suffrage (64). The Chinese and the Indians in particular came under his protective wing.

Since the days of the Gold Rush, Chinese laborers by the thousands had come to California. They worked as farmers, miners, most notably as laborers on the Central Pacific branch of the transcontinental railroad. Anti-Chinese feeling rose steadily among West Coast whites, for a variety of reasons. The most obvious of these was the inevitable shock of contact between people of sharply different cultures. The special conditions under which the Chinese came, and in which they worked and lived, heightened this instinctive xenophobia. Generally they arrived in some state of unfreedom: as indentured servants bound by credit, contract, or ticket systems of contractor control. What was more, they came not as immigrants but as sojourners—as bound laborers whose sole aim was to accumulate enough wealth to ease their lot when, as they expected, they returned to their homeland.

Demands grew that the flow of Chinese immigrants be stopped, that they be denied citizenship, that their employment be limited. More overt forms of hostility, ranging from social discrimination to mob violence, harassed the California Chinese. Nast condemned this treatment as an affront to the values of an open society—and as another expression of the Irish-Democratic viciousness that threatened Negroes in the East (65, 66, 67).

He responded also to the condition of American Indians. In the postwar years Republicans adopted Indian policies that accorded in spirit with the party's commitment to Negro civil rights. *Harper's Weekly* condemned "Our Indian Policy of Extermination" as "inhuman and unworthy of the United States." The Radical Republican Congress appointed a Peace Commission in 1867 that sought to reverse the existing policy of warfare with the Plains Indians. The first specific appropriation for Indian education came in 1870. A year later Congress adopted the Peace Commission's recommendation that the traditional treaty approach to Indian-white relations be abandoned. The Indians were to be viewed not as alien (and hostile) nations but as a minority group to be peacefully absorbed into the fabric of white American society. In 1873, President Grant adopted a "peace policy" that called on the various religious denominations to provide the teachers and Indian agents who would effect this conversion. Nast warmly approved actions so appropriate to the party of emancipation and Negro rights, and condemned those who would keep Indians apart from the diverse but unified people of the American Nation (68).

The Radical Republican concern for minority rights was an ephemeral thing, a product of the special political and ideological conditions of the war era. But Radical Republicanism drew its strength from more than the shared memory of the war. The movement for Nego rights rested in great part on a Protestant social morality that belonged to millions of Americans. Many of these people responded also to the cause of alcoholic temperance and prohibition—a cause that led a longer and more vigorous postwar life than did the appeal to human brotherhood. Massachusetts prohibitionists in 1870 spoke in a way that underlined their kinship to Radical Republicanism: "the abolition of slavery and the preservation of our Union having been accomplished, there is no issue now before the country equal to that of prohibition."

As with so many of the issues of postwar political life, prohibition-ist politics took on strong cultural overtones. Republican politicos were likely to cater to a prohibition-temperance movement rooted in the Protestant, farm and small-town population of New England and the Midwest. By the same token the Democratic party of the cities and the Irish became the natural political repository of anti-prohibition sentiment. Indiana Democrats in 1870 condemned any attempt "to regulate the moral ideas, appetites, or innocent amusements of the people by legislation."

Nast responded to the issue as yet another gauge by which to judge the state of postwar American life. He frequently commented on the degrading effects of drink, and supported a woman's temperance crusade that temporarily closed saloons in dozens of Ohio towns (69, 70).

Nast's sensitivity to social reform co-existed with a quick sympathy for postwar American business enterprise. When Wendell Phillips in 1869 attacked the Union Pacific Railroad Company, the artist lampooned him for obstructing so great a contribution to progress and national unity (71). He looked with understanding on the responsibilities of the capitalist, with distaste on attempts to establish labor unions, with horror on the specter of Communism raised by the First International and the Paris Commune (72, 73, 74). One of his notable drawings was an attack on Victoria Woodhull Claflin, who combined an untrammeled personal morality with an eccentric economic radicalism (75).

It might seem that there is a failure of sensitivity here; that an artistic conscience quick to react to political and social injustice somehow went blank when it confronted the issues posed by the economy. But closer examination of Nast's economic views suggests that they were an integral part of his Radical Republican outlook.

When business enterprise commingled with Democratic politics, as it did in the case of the Erie Railroad, Nast was ready enough to play the critic (76). But for the most part vigorous entrepreneurs belonged politically, socially, and ideologically to the Radical Republican coalition. The values central to that coalition—dedication to a unified nation, belief in social freedom and equality of opportunity, an ebullient optimism—were both useful and attractive to America's postwar entrepreneurs.

It is not surprising, then, that Nast's economic views had an intimate relationship to his general political stance. The texture of that relationship is visible in the prime economic issue of the period: the question of the nation's finances.

The exigencies of civil war led the national government to issue a billion and a half dollars' worth of legal tender treasury notes (or greenbacks), national bank notes, and government bonds. These obligations were immediately and deeply embroiled in political controversy. Were the bonds to be redeemed at their face value in gold? Should the greenbacks and bank notes be reduced in circulation? Should government specie payment be resumed for all circulating currency?

More than economic theory—and economic self-interest—shaped the debate that raged over these questions. Those who favored the resumption of specie payments on government notes and the redemption of government bonds in gold at full value identified their position with the honor of the nation; ultimately, with the cause of the Union. The national debt was one of the instruments of Northern triumph in the Civil War; to repudiate any portion of it was to dilute the victory of 1865.

Even deeper commitments underlay the support of Nast and so many of his contemporaries for a resumptionist fiscal policy. Hard money, gold-backed money had a place in mid-nineteenth-century economic thinking that was sustained by both scientific and moral considerations. Respectable political economists agreed on the viciousness of unsecured paper money. And a belief in the inalienability of credit, the sanctity of debt, had roots deep in Calvinist social thought. When Thomas Nast reacted with horror to intimations of inflation, he spoke to his Northern middle-class, Protestant readership as truly as he did on the issues of the Civil War and Reconstruction.

Nast's concern over the currency issue led him to one of his major symbolic creations: the flaccid, vacuous Rag Baby of inflation. He first used this figure to comment on Democratic division over monetary policy; hard-money leaders such as Senator Allen Thurman of Ohio and Governor Samuel J. Tilden of New York uneasily co-existed with inflationist party members (77,78). But the Rag Baby served more generally to represent a sentiment for an expanded currency that was strong in both parties during the depression-wracked 'seventies (79). It was with a special sense of triumph that Nast celebrated Grant's veto in 1874 of a bill designed to increase the circulation of legal tender and bank notes (80, 81).

The Radical Nation

The secessionist, the Democrat, the Negrophobe, the drunkard, the inflationist: all shared a social outlook that threatened the Radical Nation. They served as mutually reinforcing confirmations of Nast's view that in postwar America polar ideologies confronted each other. When he turned his attention to the relationship of the United States to the outside world, the same sense of confrontation prevailed in his work. In international no less than national affairs, Nast's primary concern was for the social values that underlay his Radical Republican creed.

[55]

PARDON.

Columbia.—"Shall I Trust These Men,

FRANCHISE.   August 5, 1865

And Not This Man?"

October 10, 1868

Patience on a Monument.

"**Halt !**"

"This is not the way 'to repress corruption and to initiate the Negroes into the ways of honest and orderly government.'"

October 17, 1874

[58]

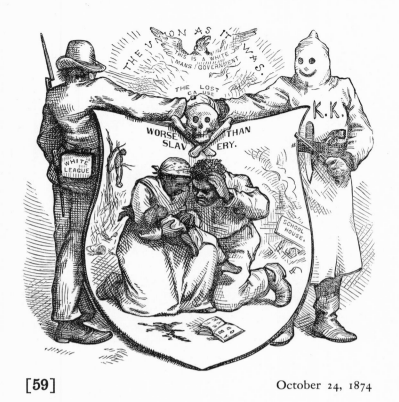

[59]

October 24, 1874

[60]

February 6, 1875

The Target

"* * * They (Messrs. PHELPS & POTTER) seem to regard the White
League as *innocent as a Target Company.*"—*Special Dispatch to the
"N.Y. Times," from Washington, Jan. 17, 1875.*

"To Thine Own Self Be True."

[61]   April 24, 1875

"These Few Precepts in Thy Memory."

Beware of entrance to a quarrel: but, being in,
Bear it that the opposer may beware of thee.
Give every man thine ear, but few thy voice:
Take each man's censure, but reserve thy judgment.
Costly thy habit as thy purse can buy,
But not express'd in fancy; rich, not gaudy:

For the apparel oft proclaims the man.

*   *   *   *   *

This above all,—To thine own self be true;
And it must follow, as the night the day,
Thou canst not then be false to any man.

SHAKSPEARE.

[62]   May 22, 1875

The "Civil Rights" Scare Is Nearly Over.
The game of (colored) fox and (white) goose.

April 3, 1875

The Good (Pure White) Shepherd.

It was known here Sunday morning that the Civil Rights Bill had passed both Houses of Congress, and needed only the signature of the President to become a law. On that very morning, in Manchester, just across the river from Richmond, a negro woman marched into the Meade Memorial Episcopal Church, just before the services began, and took a front seat beside a lady. The lady at once rose, went into the vestry-room, and informed the rector, Rev. Mr. SAMMS. Mr. SAMMS considered the situation for a few moments, and then determined that, as the easiest way out of the difficulty was perhaps the best way, he would dismiss the congregation without having any services, which he did promptly.—*New York Times.*

November 20, 1869

[64]

[65]   August 7, 1869

Pacific Chivalry.

Encouragement to Chinese immigration.

[66]   July 23, 1870

Throwing Down the Ladder by Which They Rose.

[67]

February 18, 1871

The Chinese Question.

Columbia.—"Hands off, gentlemen! America means fair play for all men."

"Move On!"

Has the native American no rights that the naturalized American is bound to respect?

April 22, 1871

[68]

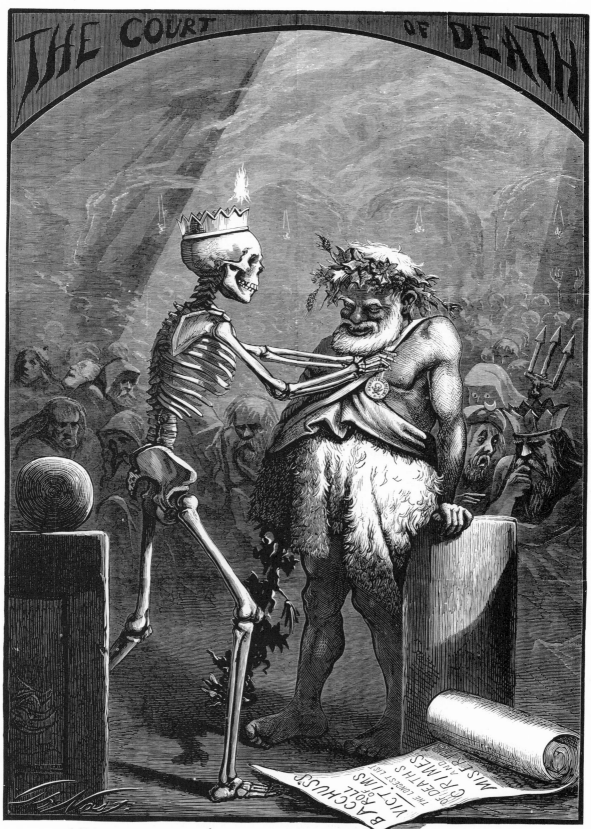

KING DEATH'S DISTRIBUTION OF PRIZES.
BACCHUS TAKES THE FIRST PREMIUM.

May 28, 1870

June 13, 1874

Jewels Among Swine.

"The police authorities, that do not enforce the laws against the liquor traffic, that
do not suppress gambling or houses of ill repute. . . . . . distinguished themselves on
Saturday by arresting forty-three women, who went on the streets to sing and pray,
and marching them to the station-house."—*Cincinnati Gazette.*

"ALL HAIL AND FAREWELL TO THE PACIFIC RAILROAD."
WENDELL PHILLIPS.

[71]

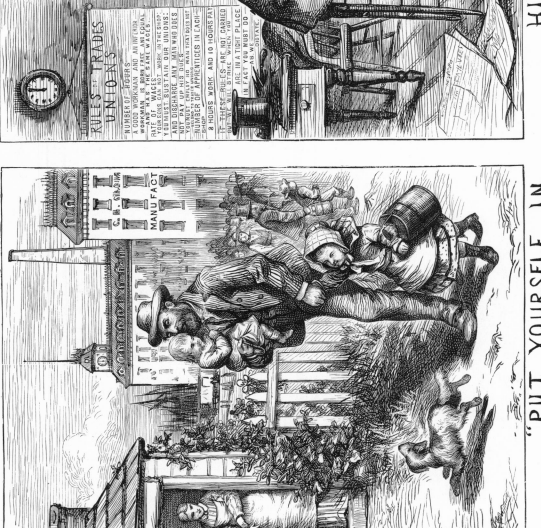

CAPITAL.

1865

RULES of TRADES
UNIONS

NUMBER OF HOURS —
A GOOD WORKMAN AND AN INFERIOR
WORKMAN IS BORN FREE AND EQUAL
AND HAS THE SAME WAGES.
RATE OF WAGES —
YOU SONS CAN NOT WORK IN THE SHOP:
YOU MUST SUSTAIN OUR UNIONS:
AND DISCHARGE ANY MAN WHO DOES
NOT PAY UP HIS DUES.
YOU MUST EMPLOY NO MAN THAT DOES NOT
BELONG TO THEIR UNION
NUMBER OF APPRENTICES IN EACH
SHOP
8 HOURS WORK AND 10 HOURS PAY
IF THESE RULES ARE NOT CARRIED
OUT WE WILL STRIKE WHEN YOU
ARE IN A TIGHT PLACE
IN FACT YOU MUST DO
AS WE
DICTATE.

CONTRACTS TO
FULFILL.

LARGE SUMS OF
MONEY AT STAKE

WAGES
EVERY
WEEK

RENT.

March 4, 1871

HIS PLACE.
"ALL IS NOT GOLD THAT GLITTERS"

AND

LABOR

MANUFACT

"PUT YOURSELF IN
"CONTENT IS HAPPINESS"

[72]

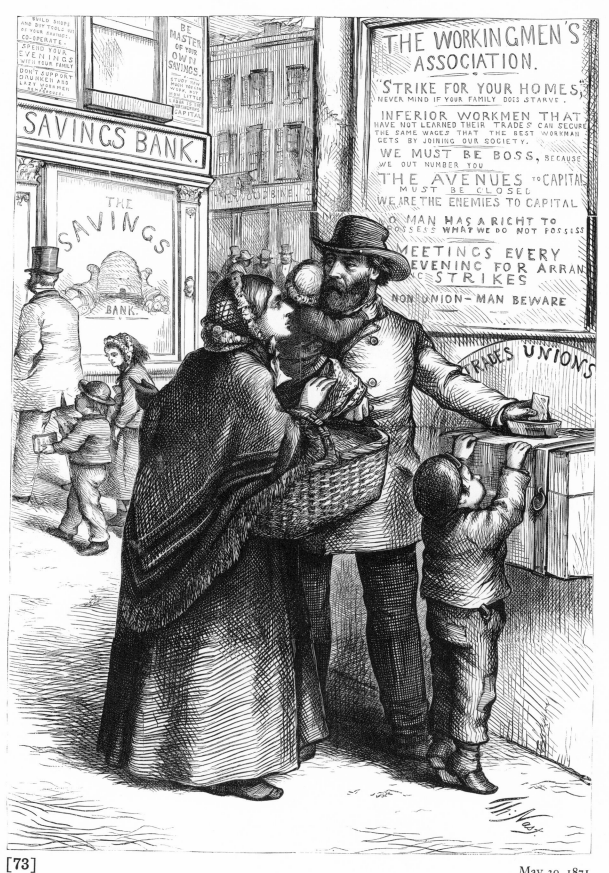

May 20, 1871

The Workingman's Mite.

February 7, 1874

The Emancipator of Labor and the Honest Working-People.

February 17, 1872

"Get Thee Behind Me, (Mrs.) Satan!"

WIFE (*with heavy burden*). "I'd rather travel the hardest path of matrimony than follow your footsteps."

March 30, 1872

Justice on the Rail—Erie Railroad (Ring) Smash Up.

September 4, 1875

That Irredeemable Rag Baby.

This is a nice position for a "hard-money" bachelor to be placed in!

October 9, 1875

"Holy Murder!!!"

Governor Tilden and the Ohio Rag Baby.

April 8, 1876

The Haunted House; or, The "Murdered" Rag Baby Will Not Be Still.

Shake its gory locks at them until they make it vanish.

May 16, 1874

A General Blow Up—Dead Asses Kicking a Live Lion.

May 23, 1874

Public Opinion—April 22, 1874.

VI
The World Outside

There had been much in the American wartime experience to encourage a postwar mood of bumptious nationalism. It was not easy to forget the hostility to the Northern cause displayed by the ruling circles of England and France. Many Americans saw the triumph of 1865 as a victory not only over secession and slavery but the aristocratic idea, over those who had awaited with high expectation the collapse of the American Republic. James Russell Lowell's Commemoration Ode of 1865 caught a mood widely current in Northern public opinion:

> Tell us not of Plantagenets,
> Hapsburgs, and Guelfs, whose thin bloods crawl
> Down from some victory in a border-brawl!
> How poor their outworn coronets,
> Matched with one leaf of that plain civic wreath
> Our brave for honor's blazen did bequeath,
> Through whose desert a rescued Nation sets
> Her heel on treason, and the trumpet hears
> Shout victory, tingling Europe's sullen ears
> With vain resentments and more vain regrets!

Secretary of State William Henry Seward sought to use this attitude as a spur to an expansionist foreign policy. He secured Alaska, and hoped to extend American control or commercial influence to a number of other locales in the Western Hemisphere. Andrew Johnson's December 1868 State of the Union message dutifully described Seward's ambitions: "Comprehensive national policy would seem to sanction the acquisition and incorporation into our Federal union of the several adjacent continental and insular communities."

But other, equally compelling consequences of the war tempered American foreign policy. The costs of the conflict encouraged the peaceful settlement of differences with Great Britain, France, and Spain. And the Radical Republican ideals of human freedom and national integrity ran counter to the expansionist impulse. It smacked too much of the slaveholding Democracy, of prewar America. Horace Greeley's *New York Tribune* warned in September 1867: "We cannot have colonies, dependencies, subjects, without renouncing the essential conceptions of domestic policy." Territorial expansion, said *Harper's Weekly*, belonged to the past as one of "the barbarities of slavery. . . . The American People, still bending under an enormous war debt, have no wish for other wars."

Thomas Nast's postwar comments on foreign affairs accurately reflected the mixed national mood of ebullience and caution. He had a ready sympathy with international developments that seemed to share the spirit of Radical Republicanism at home. He celebrated the continuing struggle for Italian unification, and welcomed the efforts of the American diplomat Anson Burlingame to bring China into closer and more amicable relations with the West (82, 83).

But when it came to the thorny topic of Anglo-American relations, his was a voice for moderation and compromise. England more than any other nation had given aid and comfort to the Confederates during the Civil War. Bitterness welled in the North particularly over the ease with which the South had commerce raiders built and fitted in Great Britain. The *Alabama* was the most successful of these corsairs. Reparations for the damage wrought by this and other ships became the central issue of British-American diplomacy during the postwar years. Charles Sumner in a notable Senate speech in April 1869 estimated that England owed the United States direct and indirect damages totaling $2,125,000,000. British opinion reacted with outraged indignation to so high an estimate of English culpability.

Nast was ready enough to puncture *Punch's* criticism of American demands (84). But his primary allegiance was to negotiation and an amicable settlement (85). Political considerations reinforced his readiness to compromise. Democrats, and that freewheeling politico Ben-

jamin Butler, appealed to Irish Anglophobia by adopting a resolutely
hostile attitude toward England (86, 87). Radical Republican spokesmen reacted accordingly. *Harper's Weekly* found a fundamental
identity of viewpoint in Gladstone's Liberals and Grant's Republicans:

> . . . there is a great party in England . . . whose political
> philosophy is that of the great party which controls the Govern-
> ment of the United States; a philosophy which not only recog-
> nizes justice and intelligence as the necessary conditions of
> national welfare, but which substantially agrees as to the methods
> by which they may best be secured.

The Grant administration, and most particularly Secretary of State
Hamilton Fish, sought a peaceful compromise. In September 1872,
an international tribunal at Geneva awarded the United States
$15,500,000 in damages. Peace through arbitration, respect for inter-
national law, at the same time a due regard for American interests:
these, thought Nast, were yardsticks of foreign policy-making appropriate to the party of progress and civilization (88, 89, 90).

The international event in the postwar years that most deeply engaged Nast's artistic and ideological sensibilities was the Franco-Prussian War. It was not difficult for him to come to a quick judgment
on the moral implications of the conflict. In his view Napoleon III
epitomized the cruel, corrupt, militaristic European overload. The
bill of indictments was a long one. In 1852 Louis Napoleon had himself crowned Emperor, thus destroying the Second French Republic.
His sympathy for the Confederacy had been undisguised, and he had
taken advantage of the Civil War to launch an ill-fated puppet empire
in Mexico.

At the same time Nast and his Republican audience warmed to a
new Germany that seemed thoroughly committed to social and economic progress, to nationalism, to an anti-papal secularism. *Harper's
Weekly* spoke of King William of Prussia "resisting, in the name of
Germany and civilization, the demand of the hereditary enemy of
liberty and Europe." Germany's cause, the magazine declared, "is
that of liberty and justice." Democratic leaders, meanwhile, reflecting
their Irish and Southern constituencies, generally championed the
French. Samuel Tilden in a speech to the 1870 New York Democratic convention attacked Bismarck and King William.

Nast castigated Louis Napoleon for bringing war to Europe (91,

92). Soon he was able to celebrate the military exploits of his homeland and of Bismarck, the architect of victory (93, 94). But his ultimate
reaction to the Franco-Prussian War transcended his sympathy for
Germany and his antipathy to the French emperor. After his first
elation over the German triumph subsided, Nast came to see the war
as a victory of chaos and unreason; the negation of progress and liberalism (95, 96). Just as the liberal and humanitarian elements of his
Radical Republican creed made him a champion of peaceful arbitration with Great Britain, so did they make him an essentially neutral
—and disapproving—observer of timeworn European power rival-
ries.

[82]   July 14, 1866

The Uprising of Italy.

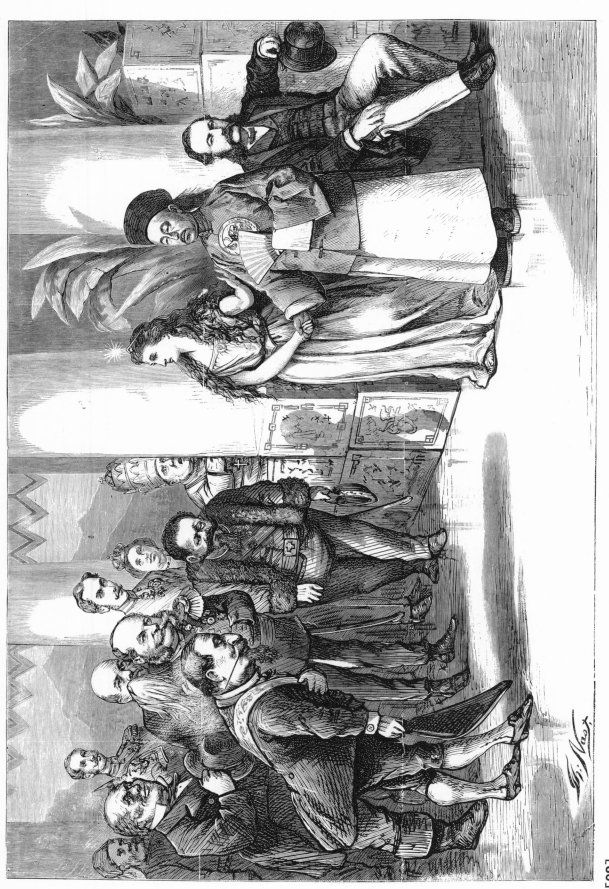

The Youngest Introducing the Oldest.

AMERICA. "Brothers and Sisters, I am happy to present to you the oldest member of the Family, who desires our better acquaintance."

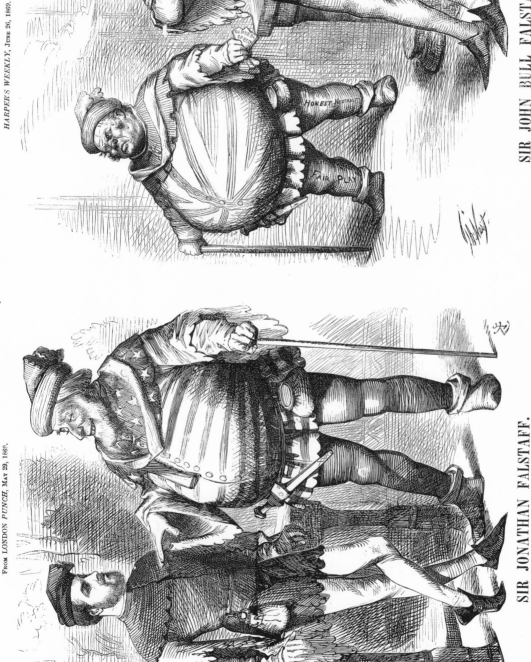

NOT "LOVE," BUT JUSTICE.

From LONDON PUNCH, MAY 29, 1869.

HARPER'S WEEKLY, JUNE 26, 1869.

[84]

SIR JONATHAN FALSTAFF.

PRINCE OF WALES. "Sirrah, do I owe you a thousand Pound?
SIR JONATHAN. "A thousand pound, Al'?—Four hundred million! Thy love is worth
four hundred million: Thou owest me thy love."—SHAKSPEARE (slightly altered).

SIR JOHN BULL FALSTAFF.   June 26, 1869.

PRINCE JONATHAN. Here comes lean Jack; here comes Barebones! How now, my sweet
creature of bombast? How long is't ago, Jack, since thou saw'st thine own knee?"
—SHAKSPEARE (not altered).

[85]

August 1, 1868

The British Lion Disarmed.

"The United States and England are united by too many bonds to make war possible; two countries may then become one in policy, as they already are, I firmly believe, but for myself I am anxious to have *every* point in dispute amicably settled, and the in sentiment and origin." —*Prince of Wales's Remarks to Mr. Bierstadt, the Artist.*

[86]   December 17, 1870

"Fe! Fo! Fi! Fum! I Smell
the Blood of an Englishman!"

[87]   May 27, 1871

The Joint High Commission.

Reconciliation of JOHN and JONATHAN.—
       Felicitations over the great Anglo-Saxon Victory.

February 24, 1872

"Well Roared, Lion," and "Well Shone, Moon!"

Lion. "You may now, perchance, both quake and tremble here,
When Lion rough in wildest rage doth roar."—SHAKSPEARE.

October 5, 1872

THE LAST
SCENE OF THE
WILLIAM TELL
TRAGEDY.

The Apple of Discord at the Geneva Tribunal.

November 4, 1874

International Law—The Better Way.

"The Nations are fast becoming so civilized as to feel that there is a better way to settle their difficulties than by fighting."—U. S. Grant.

"Who Goes There?"—"A Friend."

NAPOLÉON

"DEAD MEN'S CLOTHES SOON WEAR OUT."

[92]

September 10, 1870

C'EST LA BELLE FRANCE.

[93]

MEINE BRUST! LIEB VATERLAND

VEREINIGTEN
BAYERN
PREUSSEN
DEUTSCHL
BADEN

DAS IST DES DEUTSCHEN VATERLAND.

Th. Nast.

April 15, 1871

THROWN COMPLETELY INTO THE SHADE.

March 18, 1871

MILITARY GLORY.

November 12, 1870

DIE
WACHT AM RHEIN.

November 26, 1870

VII

The Church and the Schools

There is in Thomas Nast's work a persistent, powerful, disturbing strain of hostility to Catholics in general and to Irish-Americans in particular. It might seem paradoxical that an artist quick to respond to the cause of the underprivileged (whether Negroes, Chinese, or Indians) should be unrelentingly hostile to this substantial American minority. But Nast's anti-Catholic cartoons, like every facet of his work, had an intimate relationship to his Radical Republican point of view.

The good society of the Radical Republicans was liberal, progressive, nationalistic—and Protestant. The crusade against slavery and the war for the Union had relied heavily upon Protestant religious imagery. To Americans who were moved by these themes, the triumphant Radical Nation seemed indistinguishable from its principal religious faith. Charles Eliot Norton reflected that assumption when in 1868 he hazarded the view that Protestantism "might . . . become the complete expression, and afford the most effective organization of the moral order which underlies the political system." By the same token Roman Catholicism—a faith alien in its culture, its beliefs, the social and ethnic origins of its communicants—posed a threat to the Republic second only to that of the slaveholding, secessionist Democracy.

Nast's anti-Catholicism had roots in his German Protestant upbring-

159

ing and his intellectual coming of age at a time when anticlerical Liberalism was strong. But Papal policy and domestic events in the postwar years intensified his hostility to the Church. In December 1864—precisely when the Civil War had taken on for Nast and his audience its almost mystical significance as a struggle for human liberty and social progress—Pius IX handed down a syllabus of "the principal errors of our time." He insisted on the primacy of the Church in matters of culture, science, and education; he rejected the principle of liberty of conscience and worship; and he bluntly proclaimed: "It is an error to believe that the Roman Pontiff can and ought to reconcile himself to, and agree with, progress, liberalism, and contemporary civilization."

The Pope then consolidated his power at a Vatican Council that met from December 1869 to October 1870—the first such gathering in three hundred years. Its major work was the dogma of Papal Infallibility in matters of faith and morals. The Council thereby confirmed the judgment of Protestant—and liberal Catholic—critics that the Church was an institution hostile to the bourgeois, Liberal nationalism that had so strong a hold on public opinion in western Europe and the United States.

Bismarck in Germany, Gladstone in England, and Republican spokesmen in the United States—each in their own way—reacted adversely to the position of the Church. *Harper's Weekly*, the truest voice of Republican sentiment, indignantly observed of Pius: "In the breaking of chains, in the increase of knowledge, in the higher welfare of the greater number of human beings, in the removal of abuses, in the extinction of superstition, in the emancipation of civilization from the mortmain of ecclesiasticism, the Pope sees only the ravages of Satan." The magazine's pages in the 1870's were filled with articles detailing the evils of Catholic power abroad and at home.

Nast fully shared these sentiments. He added to old prejudices the sense that the Church posed a deadly challenge to his dearest social beliefs (97, 98). More particularly, he feared that Pius had designs on the United States (99).

Most of all, Nast worried about America's Irish Catholics. He found them ready to give a fealty to the Pope that did not exist in Europe itself (100). Domestic considerations fed his antipathy. Irish-Americans as a group had a special affinity for those aspects of American public life that he most abhorred: Negrophobia, the Democratic party.

He was not alone in his fears of a dangerous confrontation between the Irish and those white middle-class Protestants who called them-selves "Americans." *Harper's Weekly*, Horace Greeley's *Tribune*, (which spoke of the city as "New Cork"), Godkin's *Nation*—the organs of respectable opinion—dwelt on the conjunction of rising Irish and Catholic power in the United States. The New York *Times* in 1871 worriedly asked: "How Long Will Protestants Endure?"

Nast saw the Irish-Catholic threat to the separation of church and state as an issue by which the Republic, so recently threatened and preserved, once again would be tested (101, 102). Defined in this way, the theme became a potent stimulus to his artistic creativity.

Continuing Catholic-Protestant tensions gave him ample subject matter. A clash occurred on St. Patrick's Day 1867 between Irish celebrants and a Metropolitan Police Force controlled by the Re-publican legislature (103). In July 1871 the Ulster Protestant members of the Orange Society planned a parade to celebrate their national holiday. Mayor A. Oakey Hall of the Tweed Ring bowed to Irish sentiment and handed down an order forbidding the parade. A public outcry arose over this limitation on free expression, and Governor Hoffman revoked the order. The parade was held under the protec-tion of regiments of the National Guard. Numbers of Irish Catholics harried the Orangemen, and the Guardsmen opened fire; over thirty people were killed. Nast reacted to these unsettling social disturbances as he did to the issues of the Civil War and Reconstruction (104).

His anti-Catholicism was most strongly aroused by the relation-ship of the Church to public education. The New York legislature of 1868, under Democratic control, made public funds available to pri-vate—for the most part Catholic—schools and charitable institutions. And in the early 1870's Catholic complaints rose in New York, Ohio, and other states against school systems in which readings from the King James Bible were compulsory.

To Republicans of Nast's sort these were attacks on an institution central to the security and well-being of the Republic. *Harper's Weekly* spoke darkly of an "Assault upon the Citadel" by the Demo-crats and the Church: "The Democratic ring wishes to destroy the present common school system of the city, and the Romish party sup-port the attempt." Nothing was more vital to the Radical Republican sense of the good society than a flourishing public school system. By seeking public funds for sectarian schools, Catholics threatened that system—and the solidity of the national Union (105).

Nast struck out at Irish intransigence in "Miss Columbia's Public

School," and used the analogy of the firing at Fort Sumter to suggest the equivalence of the Catholic to the Confederate menace (106, 107). In what has been called the most powerful anti-Catholic cartoon ever drawn in America, he pictured Tammany and Tweed allied with the Church in a fearsome assault on the American public school (108).

It is notable that Nast's attack on the Church coincided closely in time with his great condemnation of the Tweed Ring. Each posed a threat of unusual emotional intensity to Nast's social ethos; and each evoked from him work of unusual power and passion.

PILGRIM'S PROGRESS IN THE 19TH CENTURY.

[97]

"Now I saw in my dream, that at the end of the valley lay blood, bones, ashes, and mangled bodies of men, even of Pilgrims that had gone this way formerly; and, while I was musing what should be the reason, I espied, a little before me, a cave, where two giants, Pope and Pagan, dwelt in old time, by whose power and tyranny the men, whose bones, blood, ashes, etc., lay there, were cruelly put to death. By this place Christian went without much danger, whereat I somewhat wondered: but I have learned since, that Pagan has been dead many a day; and as for the other, though he be yet alive, he is, by reason of age, and also of the many shrewd brushes that he met with in his younger days, grown so crazy and stiff in his joints, that he can now do little more than sit in his Cave's mouth grinning at Pilgrims as they go by, and biting his nails because he can not come at them.

"So I saw that Christian went on his way; yet, at the sight of the Old Man that sat in the mouth of the Cave, he could not tell what to think, especially because he spoke to him, though he could not go after him, saying, 'You will never mend till more of you be burnt!' but he held his peace, and set a good face on it, and so went by, and catched no hurt."—BUNYAN'S *Pilgrim's Progress.*

"The governments of Europe which recognize the Roman Catholic Church as the State Church, generally expect that the Council will take some new action on questions directly affecting the relation of the Church to the State, and that claims will be asserted which not a single government is likely to accept or officially to recognize."—*Daily Papers.*

EXCOMMUNICATION OF MODERN CIVILIZATION.
GALILEO OF THE 19th CENTURY. "BUT NEVERTHELESS IT DOES MOVE."

December 25, 1869

October 1, 1870

"The Promised Land," as Seen from the Dome of Saint Peter's, Rome.

[100]

America (?) Sympathizes with the Pope.

EUROPE

CHURCH & STATE

UNITED STATES. February 19, 1870

[102]

Church and State—No Union upon Any Terms.

RUM. BLOOD.

ST. PATRICKS DAY 1867.

BRUTAL ATTACK ON THE POLICE. "THE DAY WE CELEBRATE." IRISH RIOT.

Th. Nast.

April 6, 1867

[103]

HONOR TO WHOM HONOR IS DUE.

"CROPPIES LIE DOWN."

THE UPRISING OF THE PEOPLE

JULY 12TH

LIVE AND LET LIVE.

THE SLAVES OF THE

COLUMBIA SPEAKS.

What, craven fools! has't come to this, that a mob can overawe
The guardians of my children's rights, my servants clothed with law?
That they should weakly truckle, when they should be most strong,
So recreant to the cause of right, and only brave in wrong?

Abject and weak! ye trembled when firm ye should have stood,
And linked your hands in those of men whose hands are swift to blood:
Your very slaves and tools in wrong your masters have become;
They raised the sword above your head, and you were meek and dumb!

Traitors to law and Me, arise, and to the rearward stand;
It is not fit that they should rule who fear a mob's command
But first the lofty lesson learn that I am here to teach—
The rights of all my children shall be the rights of each!

The lowliest and the weakest have rights within the law
The rights of all within the law by all must be respected;
Columbia knows no difference of race, creed, or condition:
No chain upon the Conscience here of State or Inquisition!

But oh, my children, native here, or seeking here a home
From Old-World tyranny and wrong, whencever ye may come,
Can ye not learn to blend in peace, a free and happy nation,
And differ but as freemen may, with generous toleration?

The land is broad enough for all, the laws are framed to bless,
Strong to protect the rights of all, and never to oppress;
And if the rights of one may be by many trampled down,
We might as well go back to lords and ruler with a crown.

And you, if still your craven hearts can feel a manly throb,
Learn toleration don't include submission to a mob;
Go, gather up your scattered wits, and ever, from this day,
Remember that my motto is, "Give each and all fair play."

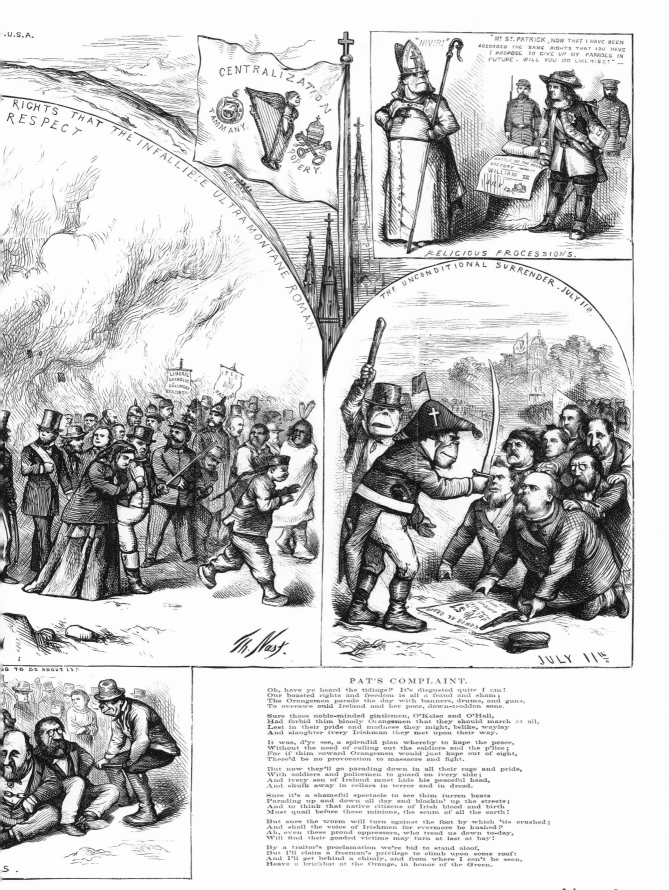

PAT'S COMPLAINT.

Oh, have ye heard the tidings? It's disgusted quite I am!
Our boasted rights and freedom is all a fraud and sham;
The Orangemen parade the day with banners, drums, and guns,
To overawe ould Ireland and her poor, down-trodden sons.

Sure those noble-minded gintlemen, O'Kelso and O'Hall,
Had forbid thim bloody Orangemen that they should march at all,
Lest in their pride and madness they might, belike, waylay
And slaughter ivery Irishman they met upon their way.

It was, d'ye see, a splendid plan whereby to kape the peace,
Without the need of calling out the soldiers and the p'lice;
For if thim coward Orangemen would just kape out of sight,
There'd be no provocation to massacre and fight.

But now they'll go parading down in all their rage and pride,
With soldiers and policemen to guard on ivery side;
And ivery son of Ireland must hide his peaceful head,
And skulk away in cellars in terror and in dread.

Sure it's a shameful spectacle to see thim furren beats
Parading up and down all day and blockin' up the streets;
And to think that native citizens of Irish blood and birth
Must quail before these minions, the scum of all the earth!

But sure the worm will turn against the foot by which 'tis crushed;
And shall the voice of Irishmen for evermore be hushed?
Ah, even these proud oppressors, who tread us down to-day,
Will find their goaded victims may turn at last at bay!

By a traitor's proclamation we're bid to stand aloof,
But I'll claim a freeman's privilege to climb upon some roof:
And I'll get behind a chimly, and from where I can't be seen,
Heave a brickbat at the Orange, in honor of the Green.

July 29, 1871

Something That Will Not "Blow Over."—July 11 and July 12, 1871.

"UNION IS STRENGTH."

DISTRIBUTION OF THE SECTARIAN FUND.

SECTARIAN BITTERNESS.

February 26, 1870

Our Common Schools as They Are and as They May Be.

[106]

November 4, 1871

THE
GOOD-FOR-NOTHING,
IN
MISS COLUMBIA'S PUBLIC SCHOOL.

DAME BRITANNIA. "Yes; the very same boy that has given me so much trouble in my school. Well, MISS COLUMBIA. *'Now you know how it is yourself!'*"

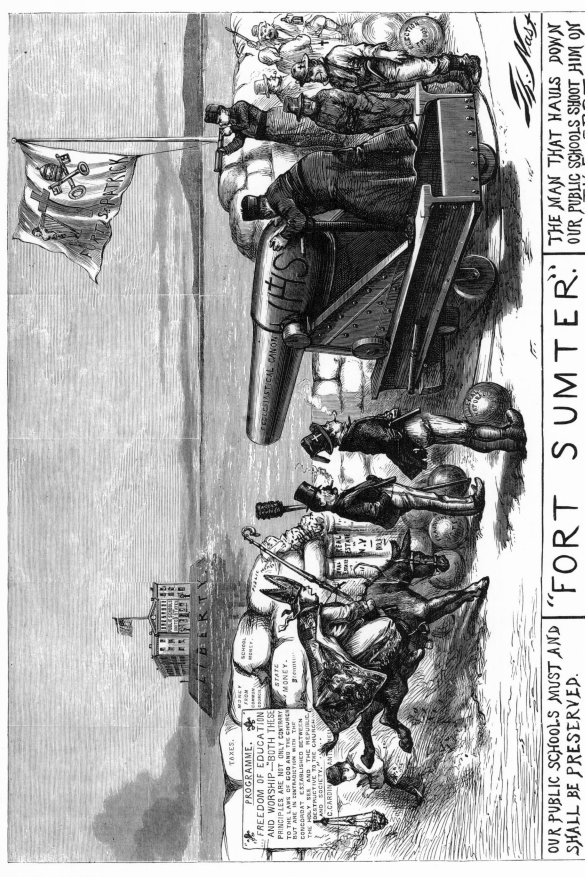

"FORT SUMTER."

OUR PUBLIC SCHOOLS MUST AND SHALL BE PRESERVED. THE MAN THAT HAULS DOWN OUR PUBLIC SCHOOLS SHOOT HIM ON THE SPOT.

March 19, 1870

[107]

THE AMERICAN RIVER GANGES.

The Priests and the Children.

September 30, 1871

[108]

VIII
Tweed

Thomas Nast's reputation rests primarily on his brilliant excoriation of the Tweed Ring. This ineffable band of politicos, who ruled Tammany Hall and New York City from 1866 to 1871, evoked Nast's most powerful work: a sustained attack which in its passion and effectiveness stands alone in the history of American graphic art. Why this should have been so is a question of some relevance to an appreciation of the wellsprings of Nast's art and to a comprehension of the political outlook to which he gave his allegiance.

Backroom manipulation of city politics by a band of professionals hardly began with William Marcy Tweed. John Adams in 1763 described a "Caucas Clubb" in Boston where "they smoke tobacco till you cannot see from one End of the Garritt to the other" and "choose a Moderator . . . select Men, Assessors, Collectors, Wardens, Fire Wards, and Representatives . . . before they are chosen in the Town." Tammany took form as the classic urban political organization in the first half of the nineteenth century. The Society of Tammany was established in 1879 as a social and patriotic club. It quickly became a force in New York politics, but for decades retained a comfortable, even an upper-class aura. Prominent merchants led the Society, which frequently displayed a nativist and anti-Catholic bias. An influx of Irish-Catholic immigrants and the democratization of

American political manners transformed the organization in the 1830's and the 1840's. The Society became the Hall: the prototypal manipulator of a city electorate, the embodiment of political venality.

Tweed, then, inherited a New York Democratic organization that already had its characteristic stamp. But there were certain qualities to Tweed's Tammany that set it apart. For the first time Irish-Catholic predominance in New York City politics was open and explicit. Tweed, though of Scotch Presbyterian origins, in personality and style was as one with the Irish pols who came to power with him, and who were to dominate the Hall from then on.

Much about this style irritated the sensibilities of Nast and his audience: the ostentation with which Tweed married off his daughter; the luxurious Americus Club where the Ring's leaders conducted lush revels; a profusion of diamonds, lavish eating and drinking; spectacular avarice (Tweed became in a few years the third largest holder of New York City real estate). Their distaste focused particularly on the Ring's baroque public thievery. Its imaginative, systematic extortion and contract padding increased New York's debt by seventy million dollars between 1869 and 1871.

In what would come to be the prevailing style of city organizations, the Tweed Ring made its avarice politically palatable by acts of conspicuous charity to its poverty-ridden constituency. Tweed gave $50,000 to aid the poor in the winter of 1870-71. Under his aegis the state legislature made appropriations to private charities; between 1869 and 1871 $2,250,000 went to (usually Catholic) schools, orphanages, and hospitals.

Conspicuous getting and spending were hardly peculiar to the Tweed Ring in the Gilded Age. But the Ring was blatant; it was Democratic; it was heavily Irish Catholic; and, most of all, it was political. It posed the greatest threat of the time to Nast's sense of the proper function of government and politics.

The semantics of the attack on the Tweed Ring are revealing. Tweed was one of the earliest American politicians to be called a "boss." And Tweed's Tammany was a pioneering city "machine" in the sense of being a permanent, all-embracing, finely articulated political organization. "Ring" in the sense of a small band of politicos also had its first widely popular usage in the case of Tweed and his associates.

There is a special metaphorical resonance to this vocabulary. It speaks of politics as an exercise in organization rather than an instrument of ideology. Tweed gave lip service to the prevalent Democratic principles of states' rights and Negrophobia; but quite obviously these —or any other—policy positions meant little to him. What mattered was the efficiency of the Machine, the solidarity of the Ring, the authority of the Boss. Tweed's associate Peter B. Sweeny noted with satisfaction at the height of the Ring's power: "The organization moves with the precision of a well-regulated machine"; and this was as much an end in itself as a means to an end.

The size of the Ring's peculations reflected the spiraling costs of a politics based on organization more than ideology. Much of the graft went to lubricate a machine that at its peak dispensed some 60,000 patronage positions. As Tweed pointed out, "The money . . . was distributed around in every way to everybody, and paid for everything, and was scattered throughout the community."

Tweed, then, was Thomas Nast's political antichrist for an interlocking set of reasons. As a Protestant, Nast was frightened by the Irish-Catholic tone of the Ring. As a Republican he was affronted by the power of this Democratic organization. As one deeply committed to a politics of morality and social purpose he was appalled by a political organization given over to nothing but its own perpetuation. The Tweed Ring challenged Nast's most profound political beliefs; and it evoked his most passionate political art.

Nast's distaste for the style of the New York Democracy predated the rise of Tweed (109). The Democratic triumph in 1869, when the party won control of the state legislature and elected John B. Hoffman governor, focused his attention on the themes of Tammany and Democratic rule. Not surprisingly, he fit the event to his already well-developed sense of Republican virtue and Democratic infamy. The triumphant New York Democracy was a threat to the beneficent Republican hegemony attained by Grant; it was the triumph of a party stained with the tar of Romanism, of corruption, or Irish drunkenness and brutality (110, 111, 112).

At first it seemed that Peter B. Sweeny, New York City Chamberlain and longtime Albany lobbyist, was the kingpin of the resurgent Democracy. But in 1870 the true configuration of the Ring emerged: "Brains" Sweeny, the manager and strategist of the combine ("I am a sort of adviser"); the clown-like, colorful front man Mayor, A. Oakey Hall (Nast's "Mayor Haul"); the skillful, corrupt comptroller and popular Irish-American leader Richard ("Slippery Dick") Connolly; and, binding it all together, the gross, forceful leader, Boss Tweed.

For some time Nast had to content himself with generalized statements on "The Fruits of the Democratic Victory," on the special Tammany commitment to political evil, on the sinister power that Tweed and Sweeny (depersonalized as "Sweed" and "Tweeny") exercised behind the throne of Governor Hoffman (113, 114, 115). By the summer of 1871 the government of New York in a new and frightening way was the province of William Marcy Tweed, the 'Brains' of a fearsomely powerful Tammany (116). But neither Nast nor anyone else had a relevant answer to the insouciant challenge of the Boss: "Well, what are you going to do about it?" (117).

In July the raw material of effective opposition came to hand. Disaffected employees of the Ring brought to the New York *Times* hard evidence of massive contract padding and other Ring frauds. The newspaper set down this corruption in incontrovertible detail. At the same time, Nast in a magnificent series of cartoons once and for all fixed the prototype of the corrupt Boss in the American political imagination.

His attack took a variety of forms. One was to comment on the particulars of the *Time's* indictment: the Ring's use of front-man contractors such as James H. Ingersoll, for example (118). He dwelt often on the ultimate victims of the Ring's frauds, the city poor whose champion Tweed claimed to be (119, 120, 121). But the true power of his work lay in his ability to cut to the heart of the moral and ideological issues raised by the Tweed Ring—and in the marriage of his indignation to a gift for ferocious caricature. His chief subjects were Sweeny, the hirsute, crafty confidante, always by Tweed's side; Hall, the pince-nezed respectable mayor; the rotund, self-satisfied Connolly; finally, towering over them—in size, in craft, in evil —the Boss himself.

Through the fall of 1871, as the state and municipal elections approached, Nast fashioned his powerful indictment. The Boss and his associates appeared as characters out of *Oliver Twist*, thieves joining in the pursuit of themselves (122). They were "A Group of Vultures Waiting for the Storm to 'Blow Over'—'Let us *Prey*' "; or wraith-like figures lamely trying to explain the unexplainable ("Too Thin!"); or frightened malefactors cowering before the gallows (123, 124, 125). Finally, on the eve of the election, Nast touched the deepest emotions of his audience with the great invention of the Tammany tiger—unleashed, rampaging in the civic arena—and return to Tweed's question: "What are you going to do about it?" (126).

Harper's circulation tripled during the course of this onslaught; bribes of hundreds of thousands of dollars were offered—as were threats such as cancellation of the city's order of Harper Brothers' textbooks. E. L. Godkin's *Nation* declared: "Mr. Nast has carried political illustrations during the last six months to a pitch of excellence never before attained in this country, and has secured for them an influence on opinion such as they never came near having in any country." Less graciously, but no less genuinely, Tweed observed: "I don't care a straw for your newspaper articles, my constituents don't know how to read, but they can't help seeing them damned pictures."

The election ran heavily against Tweed in the city and the Democrats in the state. Nast once again savored the special satisfaction of the artist who has had a share in shaping public events. Tweed and Tammany seemed sunk in ruin—as always, a premature supposition (127, 128). More important, the American Republic had shown the world (as in 1865) that democracy could cleanse itself of evil (129).

What followed was less vivid, less compacted, less satisfactory. Two years of trials and investigations yielded mixed results. Sweeny and Connally fled the country; Mayor Hall came to trial but was acquitted; Tweed's first court appearance ended in a mistrial. Nast worried over the Ring's seeming immunity to successful prosecution (130). He was disturbed too when Horace Greeley, anxious for Democratic support in his quest for the Presidency, spoke of a reformed Tammany (131, 132).

But Tweed's power was not to be restored. The Boss was sentenced to twelve years in prison in November 1873. Democratic professionals—Governor Hoffman, Samuel J. Tilden—turned against his organization (133, 134). Nor did a supposedly reformed Tammany Hall fare well in the state and city elections of 1875 (135).

In January 1875 it appeared that Tweed might be let out of jail by the payment of a token fine. But a civil suit to recover six million dollars in stolen municipal funds kept him in prison. The lawyer David Dudley Field led Tweed's defense in these proceedings. Nast turned with fury on Field (who dabbled in Democratic politics and had represented the Gould-Fisk Erie combine): the law, like politics, was too important a part of the Sacred Republic to be abused (136, 137, 138, 139). Tweed escaped from jail at the end of 1875, and hid in New Jersey while a jury finally brought in a verdict for the recovery of the six million. At that point he fled the country. Finally he was apprehended in Spain—by authorities who identified him with the aid of a Nast cartoon (140). Tweed was returned to jail, and died there in April 1878.

But of course Tammany did not die—nor did the political evolution in which Tweed played so conspicuous and tawdry a part. Tweed and his Ring represented, in their raw and corrupt way, a politics of organization and patronage that rapidly replaced the politics of ideology—and passion—of the Civil War era. Variants of Tweed were at work in other cities, in state organizations, in both parties, effecting the stylistic and organizational accommodations that would, before the 1870's were over, change the face of American political life. As his great series of Tweed cartoons revealed, Nast could react to these political changes with verve and fire. But soon they affected his own Republican party as well as the hated Democrats; and in a new milieu Nast's political art began to lose its relevance.

February 9, 1867

December 4, 1869

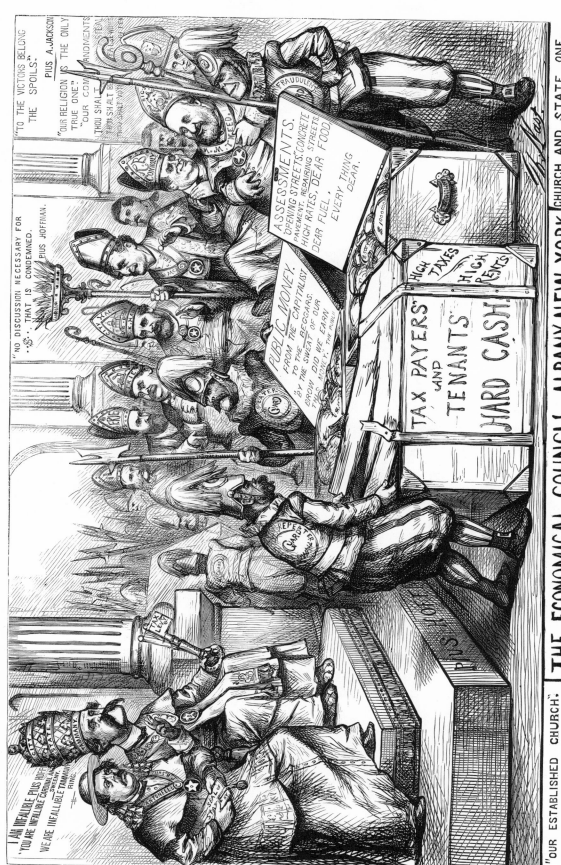

"OUR ESTABLISHED CHURCH." | THE ECONOMICAL COUNCIL, ALBANY, NEW YORK. | CHURCH AND STATE ONE.

"THE GOOD COUNSEL I CAN COMMAND IN MY SPHERE." PIUS "HOFFMAN I.

[111]

December 25, 1869

THE GREEK SLAVE.

April 16, 1870

EXCELSIOR.

January 22, 1870

June 4, 1870

THE POWER BEHIND THE THRONE.

HE CANNOT CALL HIS SOUL HIS OWN.

Th. Nast

October 29, 1870

[116]   October 21, 1871

The "Brains."

THE BOSS. "Well, what are you going to do about it?"

[117]   August 19, 1871

Under the Thumb.

That achieved the Tammany victory at
the Rochester Democratic Convention.

TWO GREAT QUESTIONS.   Th. Nast

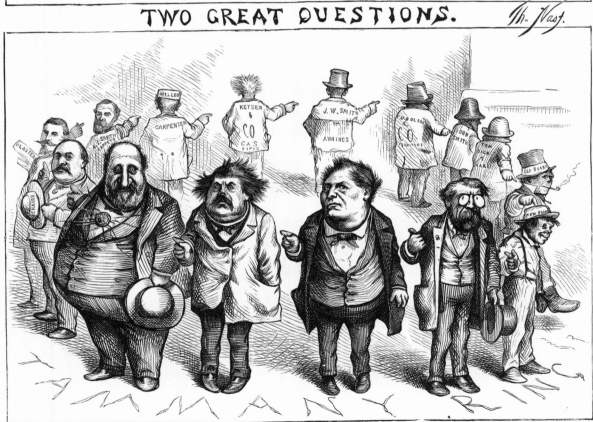

"WHO STOLE THE PEOPLE'S MONEY?" — DO TELL. N.Y. TIMES.   'TWAS HIM.

THE BED OF ROSES.

"THE RICH GROWING RICHER, THE POOR GROWING POORER."

"—WE DRINK TO OUR CONSTITUENTS. MAY THEY LIVE LONG, SO THAT WE MAY. PROSPER."

—"YES. THE RENT IS "PERHAPS EXORBITANT" BUT YOUR HUSBAND ALWAYS VOTES FOR THE VERY MEN WHO MAKE EVERY THING "PERHAPS EXORBITANT."

BRINGING THE THING HOME.

BED OF THORNS.

September 2, 1871

The Tammany Lords and Their Constituents.

WHOLESALE.

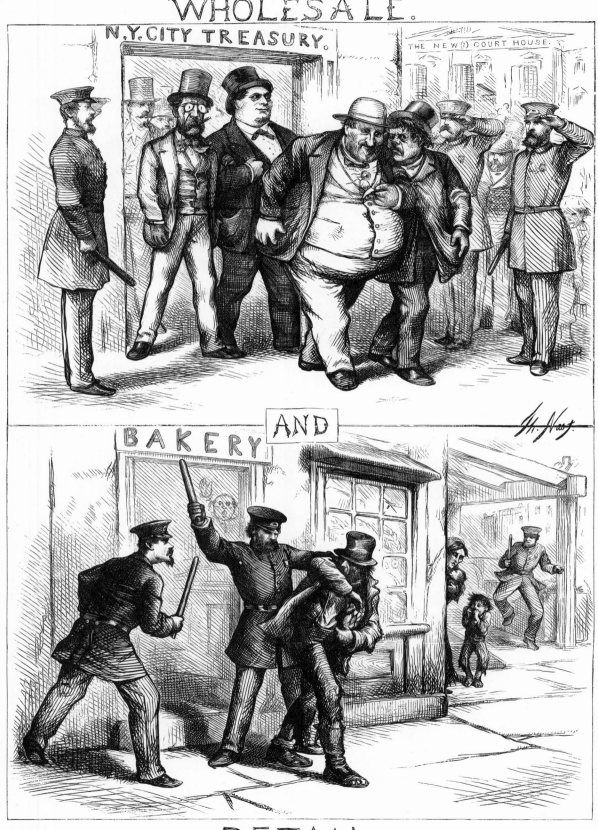

[120]   RETAIL.   September 16, 1871

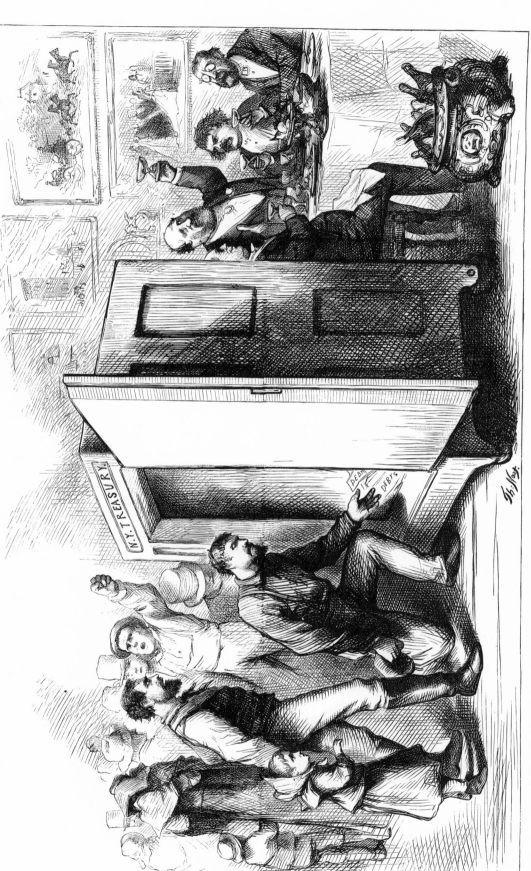

EMPTY.   FULL.

"WHAT ARE YOU GOING TO DO ABOUT IT?"

EMPTY TO THE WORKMEN.   THE FOUR MASTERS THAT EMPTIED IT.

The City Treasury.

October 14, 1871

[121]

October 7, 1871

"Stop Thief!"

"They no sooner heard the cry, than, guessing how the matter stood, they issued forth with great promptitude; and, shouting "Stop Thief!" too, joined in the pursuit like *Good Citizens*."—Oliver Twist."

September 23, 1871

**A Group of Vultures Waiting for the Storm
To "Blow Over."—"Let Us Prey."**

"WE KNOW NOTHING ABOUT "TOO THIN!" "WE ARE INNOCENT."
THE STOLEN VOUCHERS."

[124]

September 30, 1871

[125]

October 21, 1871

The Only Thing They Respect or Fear.

"We presume it is strictly correct to say that the one consequence of thieving which ——would now dread is a violent death. Public scorn, or even the penitentiary, has little terrors for them.

"We do not know how the affair may end, but we do know that if——close their careers in peace, and ease, and affluence, it will be a terrible blow to political and private morality."—*The Nation.*

[126]

The Tammany Tiger Loose.

November 11, 1871

——"What Are You Going To Do About It?"

[127]

November 25, 1871

"What Are You Laughing at? To The Victor Belong The Spoils."

Something That Did Blow Over—November 7, 1871.

[129]   December 2, 1871

To Whom It May Concern.

NEW YORK. "Now you see what I did about it. Go and do likewise."

December 23, 1871

The Dead Beat.

The Ghost of Dick Turpin to Jack Sheppard. "There's no use talking. To them belongs the palm. They have completely outdone us."

August 10, 1872

The Cat's Paw.—Any Thing To Get Chestnuts.

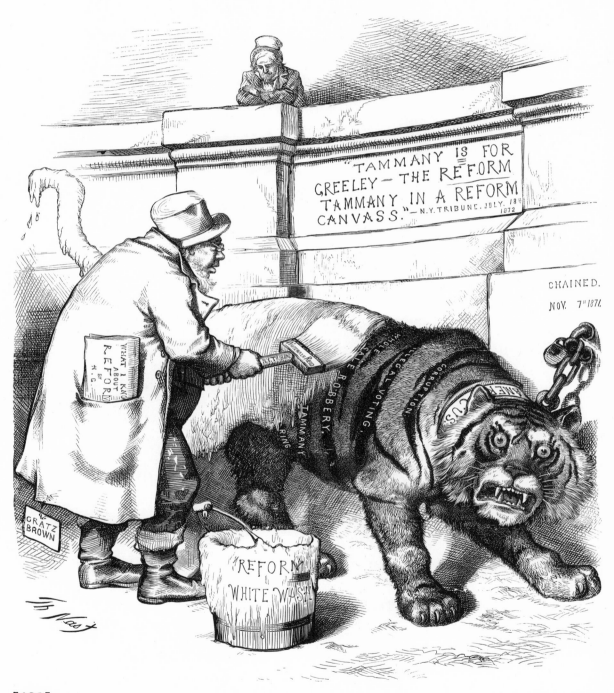

August 31, 1872

"What Are You Going To Do About It,"
If "Old Honesty" Lets Him Loose Again?

January 27, 1872

"Et Tu, Brute?—Then Fall, Caesar."

"Though the Charter was not all it should have been, it was the best that could then be obtained, and it promised relief from great and long-continued wrong, under which the people of the City had been suffering, and from a system of government the abuses under which are now coming to light. The misconduct recently exposed was not a consequence from any of its provisions.

"The responsibility for the wrong-doing which has very justly aroused public indignation does not rest so much upon the Charter as upon individuals who held office in the City before the Charter was passed, and took office also under it.

"The complaints with regard to the late election in New York and Brooklyn, made through the Press, are chiefly of false counting of ballots and false returns by inspectors of election. The general suspicion of the existence of such an evil is almost as injurious as the practice itself: our people, if led to believe that it is carried on extensively, will neglect to vote, and will lose their habit of submitting quietly to the result of an election. The crime is, under our form of government, one of the worst, in its nature and in its effects, and should be punished accordingly. It is a practice which, if persisted in, is more likely to overturn our Government than any open war that can be levied against it. Effectual laws against bribery of the electors, and to take away an office obtained by bribery, thorough protection of the right of challenge on election day, severe penalties against miscounting of votes and against illegal voting, ought to suffice for the protection of the ballot, and will suffice if citizens, juries, and public officers will do their duty."—GOVERNOR HOFFMAN'S MESSAGE, 1872.

November 7, 1874

A Tammany Rat.

TAMMANY'S WATERLOO.

THE DEMOCRATIC MAJORITY IN NEW
YORK STATE REDUCED 40,000.

REPUBLICAN MAJORITY IN BOTH HOUSES
OF THE LEGISLATURE.

INDEPENDENCE ON THE BENCH.

CRUSHING DEFEAT OF BOSS KELLY.

OVER 20,000 MAJORITY FOR HACKETT AND
PHELPS, THE PEOPLE'S CANDIDATES.

REPUBLICAN VICTORIES IN
PENNSYLVANIA,
MASSACHUSETTS,
MINNESOTA,
NEW JERSEY,
and KANSAS.

[135]

November 20, 1875

Tammany Down Again—The "Reform" Trap Smashed.

August 7, 1875

Princip-als, Not Men—A Lawyer Pleading for His "Client."

[137]

January 15, 1876

The (D.D.) Field of Gold, or the Lion's Legal(?) Share.

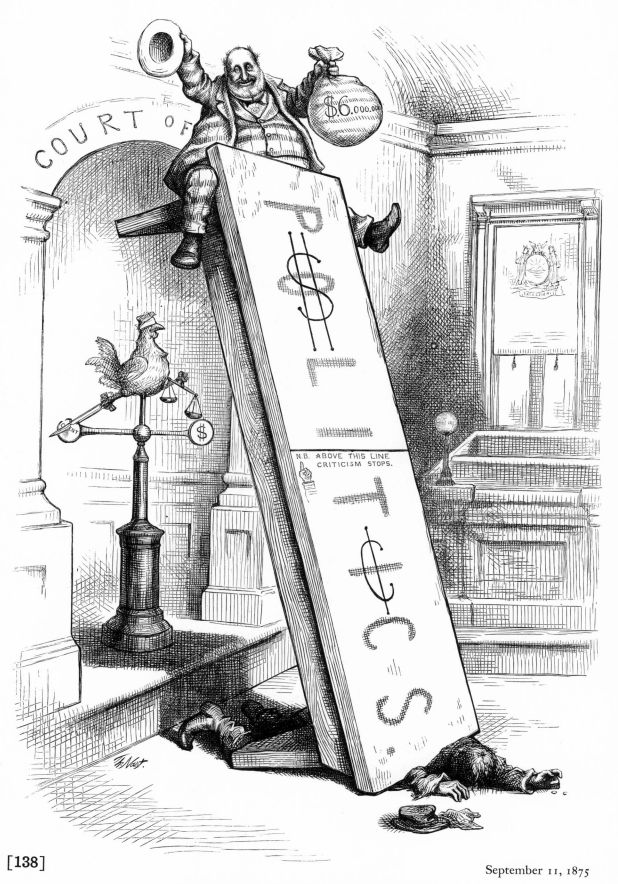

September 11, 1875

"The Upright Bench," Which Is Above Criticism.

ICH DIEN.

FISK, GOULD,
TWEED, TILDEN.

D. D. FIELD.
LAWYER.

[139]

February 24, 1877

They Do Each Other Honor.

Mr. ***** (*the Most Ancient Fraud*). "Your *fame* has reached beyond this *cold world*, and I have come to ask you to defend *Me*."

POLITICAL "CAPITAL."

The "people are in a very puzzled and despondent state of mind about the political situation, and have got beyond the point at which they look for the appearance of the ideal statesman uniting the purest motives with the highest ability. They can get the pure motives, and they can get the high ability; but somehow, owing to no matter what circumstances, to get a man who unites both into a leading place in the government is a work of such difficulty that most people have given it up as (for the present at least) a bad job, and are willing to content themselves with any man who, for whatever motive, will do good work. It so happens, too, that the work to be done at this moment is not work which calls either for the highest order of genius or the highest aspirations. A man may do it very well without being a Moses or a Washington—without, in short, being either a prophet or a hero. He has neither to lead a race out of captivity nor call a nation into existence. The task before the American politician of to-day is the simple and somewhat homely one of preventing public officers from stealing and dividing the public money, and of preventing the government from cheating its creditors; and when a man offers himself for this work, there is no general disposition to ask whether he is a statesman of the first rank, or whether his political judgment has always been sure or his voice been always heard on the right side. In fact, they go so far as to say that to make capital in this way is a good thing to do, and they wish all politicians to engage in it. They are ready to forbear all curious inquiries into the motives or antecedents of men who will undertake to put an end to cheating and stealing. In fact, the voters of the country are sticking notices up offering the highest offices in their gift, and "no questions asked," to any body who will bring in a few plunderers of the state. Mr. Tilden has achieved his present success simply owing to his having, before any body else of his class, understood the exact nature of the situation. He perceived sooner than his competitors that the time had come to stop preaching, and to begin making arrests and drawing up indictments. He now finds, and his competitors find, that his acuteness has rendered him the highest service, and his enemies actually play into his hands."—*The Nation, October 7, 1875.*

October 7, 1876

The Capture of Tweed—The Picture That Made the Spanish Officials Take Him for a "Child-Stealer."

IX

The Decline of the Radical Spirit:
Minorities

Radical Republicanism as a political and social force in American life flourished only for a brief span of years: from the end of the Civil War to the early 1870's. From then on time and events eroded its influence. The Republicans would not for decades win so sharp and decisive a political victory as they did in 1872. The harsh depression that began in 1873 and continued almost to the end of the decade weakened both the popularity and the *élan* of the GOP. The failures of Radical Reconstruction nourished a national predisposition toward racist attitudes.

The Radical political decline coincided with, and was sustained by, a changed tone to American intellectual life. The optimistic nationalism of the Civil War era gave way to doubts about the moral worth of the society. E. L. Godkin's *Nation*, created in 1865 to carry on into postwar America the abolitionist spirit of Radical reform, became in the 'seventies the voice of the Mugwump: querulous, frustrated, disillusioned. Political novels of the 'seventies—Mark Twain and Charles Dudley Warner's *The Gilded Age*, Henry Adams's *Democracy*— looked cynically at a party life that appeared to have no purpose but its own perpetuation. John W. DeForest's *Honest John Vane* (1874), an ironic examination of the corruption of a young Congressman, suggests the new mood. Vane tells an older colleague: "I thought general legislation was the big thing, . . . reform, foreign relations, sectional questions, constitutional rights, and so on." "All exploded, my dear sir!" was the response. "All dead issues, as dead as the war. Special legislation . . . is the sum and substance of Congressional business in our day."

In the 1860's the most influential American intellectuals had been excited by the vision of the triumphant, uplifted, purified American Republic. Now with comparable unanimity they found the Republic marred by corruption and decay. James Russell Lowell morosely commemorated the nation's centennial in 1876 in "The Land of Broken Promise":

> Show 'em your Civil Service and explain
> How all men's loss is everybody's gain;
> Show your new patent to increase your rents
> By paying quarters for collecting cents;
> Show your short cut to cure financial ills
> By making paper dollars current bills;
>
> . . .
>
> Show your State Legislature; show your Rings,
> And challenge Europe to produce such things
> As high officials sitting half in sight
> To share the plunder and to fix things right.

Thomas Nast inevitably commented on—and eventually shared—this change of spirit. The transformation of his outlook was considerably slower, and perhaps more painful, than that of other influential voices in American life. As late as 1876 he had a suggestive clash with editor George W. Curtis when he prepared a Centennial cartoon that stressed America's superiority to the corrupt Old World. Curtis disapproved of the drawing's message, and kept it out of *Harper's Weekly*. But gradually Nast's optimism and openness gave way to a more skeptical, a less ebullient view.

Causes that once had been important and deeply felt parts of the Radical Republican social outlook came to be empty and mechanical as the 1870's wore on. Nowhere was this process more evident than in that always tenuous and sensitive area of Radical Republican attitudes, the place of minorities in American life.

Radical Republican anti-Catholicism persisted—but it was based more and more on overt political self-interest, less and less on a felt social reality. Although clashes over the Catholic relationship to public education continued to occur—in Illinois, Missouri, Ohio, Connecticut—the issue did not retain the immediacy and force that it had when it arose in Tweed's New York. The Church itself seemed to be declining in militancy: the papacy in 1878 entered into the more progressive era of Leo XIII.

But important elements in Nast's party—and Nast himself—continued to act as though the Republic was in danger (141). In October 1875 President Grant called on the veterans of the Army of the Tennessee to "keep the church and the state forever separate" so that every child might have "the opportunity of a good common-school education, unmixed with sectarian, pagan or atheistical dogmas." Grant darkly predicted: "If we are to have another contest in the near future of our national existence, I predict that the dividing line will not be Mason's and Dixon's, but between patriotism and intelligence on the one side, and superstition, ambition, and ignorance on the other." The 1876 Republican platform endorsed James G. Blaine's proposal for a Constitutional amendment forbidding government aid to sectarian schools, and spoke of the public school as "the bulwark of the American republic." Nast dwelt on the issue during the 1876 campaign (142, 143). But this was only the resurrection of a shopworn theme by a party long in office and short on new political dialogue. After the election neither Nast nor his party paid further attention to a Catholic threat to American institutions.

The more generous Radical Republican tradition of tolerance toward American racial minorities—Chinese, Indians, Negroes—persisted in Nast's art. But increasingly his was a minority voice; and gradually he came to accept the prevailing attitudes of his time.

The hard times of the 1870's fed an already vigorous anti-Chinese sentiment in California. San Francisco labor leader Denis Kearney organized a Workingman's party in 1877. He harangued his constituency with an inflammatory rhetoric directed against bankers, railroad executives and, with special venom, the Chinese. Political pressures for Chinese exclusion had their effect on the Republican party too. The Hayes administration negotiated a new treaty with China in 1880 that gave the United States the power to limit Chinese immigration. In 1882 a bipartisan Congressional coalition passed a bill suspending this traffic for twenty years. President Chester Arthur vetoed so flagrant a repudiation of established Republican—and national—immigration policy. But Congress quickly passed a revised bill putting a ten-year halt to Chinese immigration, and Arthur accepted it as a face-saving compromise. An old tradition of free access to the

United States had been breached. Nast sharply criticized this suggestive turn from the social policies of the Radical years (144, 145, 146).

Yet he himself shared the growing ambivalence of his party and his generation toward racial equality in the United States. Nast's support of Indian assimilation and citizenship was affected by the sinuosities of party politics. When the Democratic House sought to reduce army appropriations, he opposed the policy by appealing to anti-Indian sentiment (147). Carl Schurz, Hayes' Secretary of the Interior, attempted to take Indian affairs from the War Department's jurisdiction. Nast had an antipathy to Schurz dating back to the Liberal Republican days of 1872, and he had a special feeling for the Army of the Union. Again he used Indian savagery as a device for criticizing a political enemy (148).

But at the same time he praised the civilizing force of citizenship and the ballot, and retained a sympathy for the underdog that led him to look upon Indians, Negroes, and Chinese as the common victims of racism and xenophobia (149, 150). His inconsistency may be taken as a measure of the ideological strain imposed on him by the changing political and intellectual environment. Only a few years before his social outlook had been consistent and coherent; now it was shaken, distorted, ultimately to be transformed.

The most revealing measure of this transformation was the collapse of the Republican commitment to Negro civil rights. Nast continued in the late 'seventies to comment acidly on Democratic intentions and actions toward the Negro. Southern promises of fair treatment in exchange for Negro votes were not to be trusted; the party remained a compound of unregenerate Rebels and Negrophobic Irishmen (151, 152).

He could not ignore the fact that his own party's concern for Negro civic equality was fading fast. Nast took Republicans to task for failing to compensate the stricken depositors of the Freedman's Bank, a venture typical of the high noon of Radical Republicanism which—typically—fell victim to peculation and the panic of 1873 (153). And he found it hard to accept Hayes's "Southern Policy" of 1877-78, an ill-favored attempt to weld an alliance of Whiggish white Southerners and like-thinking Northern Republicans. Under pressure from the editor and publisher of *Harper's* he withheld comment on that policy, and wryly commented on his own silence (154).

The conditions that eroded the postwar movement for Negro rights ultimately affected Nast's frame of reference too. *Harper's*

Weekly in the mid-1870's began to print Sol Ettinge's condescending drawings of Negro life—classic stereotypes of a carefree people happy in their simplistic ignorance. Nast was increasingly inclined in the decade's later years to portray Negroes unfavorably when it served a political purpose. He equated the Irish of the North and the Negroes of the South as "the ignorant vote" (155). When James G. Blaine, in full pursuit of the Presidency, favored the restriction of Chinese immigration, Nast took caustic note: but his device was to compare the Chinese and the Negroes to the disfavor of the latter (156).

After 1880 Nast all but ignored the continuing political and social repression of Southern Negroes. Instead he echoed the prevailing assumptions of respectable opinion in the North: that a New South had appeared, dedicated not to racism but to productivity and hard work; that Negro rights had become nothing more than the device of cynical politicians; that those who dwelt on the ill treatment of Negroes (as did Whitelaw Reid of the *New York Tribune*) were belaboring "A Dead Issue" (157, 158, 159). The Radical Republican commitment to Negro civil equality, in ideological resonance second only to the preservation of the nation, had run off into insignificance.

GOVERNMENT
OF THE PEOPLE,
BY THE PEOPLE,
FOR THE PEOPLE,
SHALL NOT PERISH
FROM THE
EARTH

THE
TIGRESS
PROTECTING HER
CUBS.

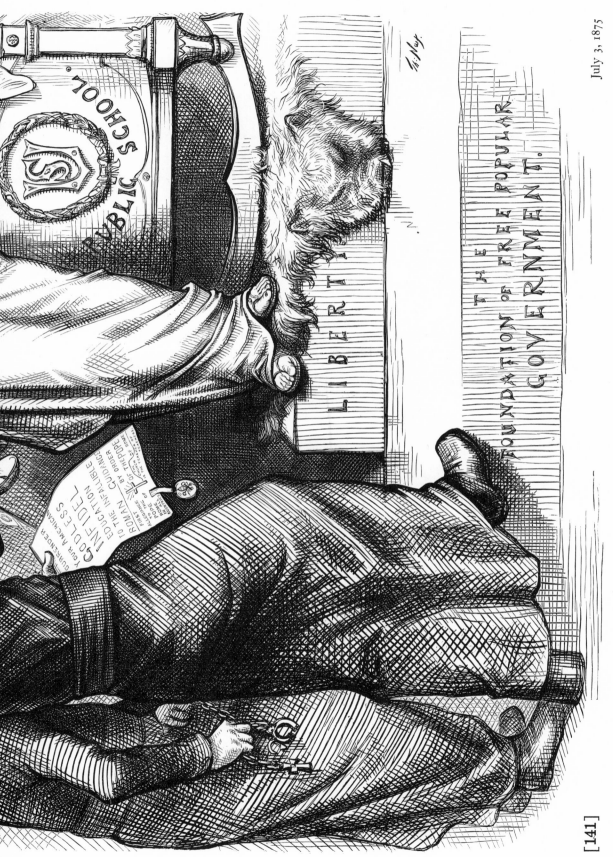

Beware!

July 3, 1875

October 23, 1875

The Plank—Hitting the Nail on the Head.

September 16, 1876

Tilden's "Wolf at the Door, Gaunt and Hungry."—Don't Let Him In.

[144]   March 25, 1872

Which Color Is To Be Tabooed Next?

FRITZ (to Pat). "If the Yankee Congress can keep the *yellow* man out, what is to hinder them from calling us *green* and keeping us out too?"

[145]   April 1, 1882

E Pluribus Unum (Except the Chinese).

Th. Nast.

May 20, 1882

(Dis-) "Honors Are Easy."

Now both parties have something to hang on.

K K
DEMOCRATIC
REVOLUTIONARY
HOUSE
A
WHOLESALE SLAUGHTER
BY THE SIOUX.
OF OUR SOLDIERS,
THE NUMBER OF KILLED AT 300.
AND THE WOUNDED AT 31.
THE INDIANS WILL
REDUCE
OUR SKELETON ARMY
STILL MORE.
WAR DEP
ORDER
TEN BALL CARTR DGES PER MONTH
FOR TARGET PRAC TICE
ALL INDIANS WILL PLEASE
KEEP OFF THE RESERVATION
AS THE AM UNITION IS EXHAUSTED
AND THE ARMY BEING
REDUCED.
Th: Nast.

[147] July 29, 1876

The New Alliance.

"We stand here for retrenchment, and *reducing the Army of the United States.*"

[148]

December 28, 1878

Patience Until the Indian Is Civilized—So To Speak.

SECRETARY OF THE INTERIOR. "There are two methods of Indian management possible: either to herd and coral the Indians under the walls or guns of a military force, so to speak, so as to watch them and prevent outbreaks; or to start them at work upon their lands, to educate them, and to civilize them. . . . There are in the Army a great many gentlemen who have good ideas about the Indian Service, but it is one thing to have ideas, and another to carry them out, and I think that the patient labor and care of detail necessary to raise the Indian tribes to a state of civilization would not be found among the officers of the Army."

March 13, 1880

Give the Natives a Chance, Mr. Carl.

The cheapest and quickest way of civilizing them.

[150]

February 8, 1879

"Every Dog" (No Distinction of Color) "Has His Day."

RED GENTLEMAN TO YELLOW GENTLEMAN. "Pale face 'fraid you crowd him out, as he did me."

May 31, 1879

Another Step Toward Civilization.

Mr. Solid Brutus. "Why, Mr. Exode Caesar, you are a Man and a Brother after all.
So step into my parlor."

October 23, 1880

**"Freedom of Suffrage to the Blacks Means Freedom
of Suffrage to the Whites."—Evarts.**

SOLID SOUTH. "Hurry up, dough-face, and shut up your side. Mine is *solid*."

[153]

March 29, 1879

Waiting.

A debt that the Republican Party ought to wipe out.

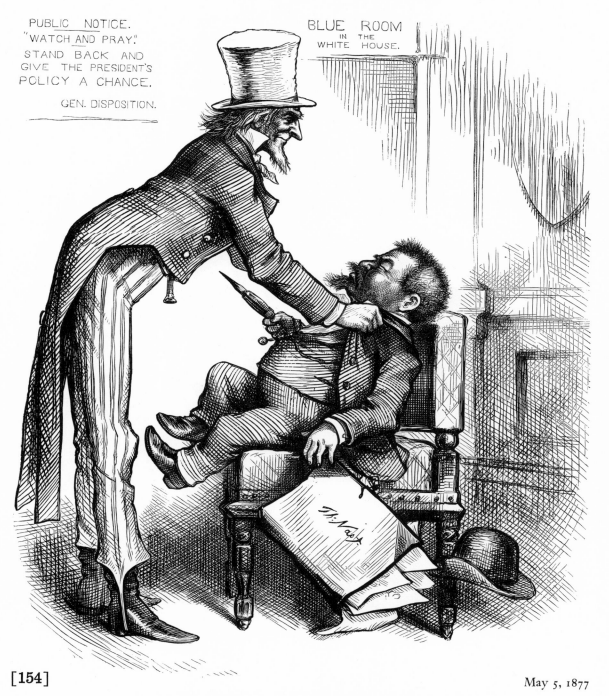

May 5, 1877

"Nay, Patience, or We Break the Sinews."—Shakspeare

U. S. "Our artist must keep cool, and sit down, and see how it works."

December 9, 1876

The Ignorant Vote—Honors Are Easy.

March 8, 1879

The Civilization of Blaine.

JOHN CONFUCIUS. "Am I not a man and a brother?"

January 14, 1882

The Queen of Industry, Or, The New South.

[158]

July 25, 1885

The "Practical" Politician's Love for the Negro.

[159]   August 29, 1885

A Dead Issue.

SOUTH. "I should like to oblige you by killing a few
negroes, Mr. Tribune, but I am too busy."

X

The Decline of the Radical Spirit:
Economic and Foreign Policy

From 1873 to 1878 the United States was in the grip of industrial depression. Those who suffered most from hard times—the poor, the unskilled, the unemployed—remained mute. But more substantial groups, whose deprivation seemed greater because they had so much more to lose, turned to political and social protest. Farmers and, for the first time, significant numbers of workingmen joined in a movement for currency inflation. And the grievances of industrial workers occasionally burst out in strikes and violence.

Thomas Nast reacted to these expressions of economic distress with passionate hostility. In one sense, his attitude was not new. He always equated the interests of labor with those of capital; looked on inflationist schemes as threats both to national honor and rational economic policy; viewed economic radicalism as a form of treason comparable to secession.

But before the mid-'seventies these views were subordinated to the sturdy optimism of his Radical Republicanism. Now, as his faith in the Republican party—and in the soundness of American life—began to weaken, his became a shriller voice. He reacted to economic protest with an intensified fear and dislike. The commanding ideal of Nast's life and art—the unified, free Republic—was threatened by the assumption that now there were two nations, the rich and the poor.

243

The movement against the resumption of specie payments came to a climax in the late 1870's. Greenback, Independent, and Anti-Monopoly tickets figured prominently in state and local politics. In 1876 an Independent Greenback ticket headed by Peter Cooper contested the Presidency. The party's platform summed up the soft money position. It demanded the repeal of the Specie Resumption Act of 1875, which pledged the government speedily to resume specie payments on outstanding notes and currency; it called for the issue of new, low-interest government notes to serve as additional currency; and it objected to the sale of gold-backed government bonds abroad.

Nast remained profoundly committed to the principle that these policies were immoral (160). But he had to face the fact that prominent figures in his own party supported a greenback currency. These included Western Republican Senators Oliver Morton of Indiana and John Logan of Illinois, and a few Eastern Congressmen: William O. Kelley of Pennsylvania, who served his industrial constituency by calling for a high tariff and easy money (161), and Benjamin Butler, who in 1874 sought the United States Senatorship from Massachusetts as a spokesman of soft money and labor reform (162).

Particularly disturbing to Nast was the rise of Republican sentiment for a bimetallic currency: the first stages of a silverite movement that would occupy the center of the political stage by the 1890's. In 1878 Senator Stanley Matthews of Ohio—a major figure in the negotiations that settled the Hayes-Tilden election crisis—offered a resolution that made silver legal tender for the payment of government bonds. The Senate passed the resolution; and Nast brilliantly transmuted "St. Matthews" into a trap that had ensnared an unwary Uncle Sam (163). But the widespread indifference to fundamental precepts of financial integrity only reinforced his fear that something vital had gone out of the national fiber (164).

Similar considerations shaped Nast's response to the issue of the income tax. Established in 1861 as a wartime revenue measure, the tax (never an onerous one) was repealed in 1872. In the late 'seventies, Greenbackers and other economic protestants of the West and South called for its return. But the artist saw the income tax as yet another device by which a decreasingly trustworthy political order might disturb the economy (165, 166).

Nast's burgeoning social fears appeared most clearly in his commentary on the industrial unrest and agitation of the time. Violence fostered by the Molly Maguires flared through the Pennsylvania coal fields in the mid-'seventies; in 1877 major railroad strikes brought rioting to several cities; in 1878 the Knights of Labor was organized as a national industrial union. Both Marxian socialism and anarchism gained a foothold on the fringes of American industrial life. The Socialist Labor party was organized in 1876-77; and in the early 1880's believers in radical propaganda by the deed of violence—Albert Parsons, August Spies, Johann Most—settled in Chicago.

"Communism" and "internationalism" served Nast as symbols of the dangers besetting American workmen—and American society—in the late 'seventies (167, 168, 169, 170). He was not alone: the fear of violent social revolution had begun to play on the minds of large numbers of middle-class Americans. The Paris Commune of 1871—vividly and unfavorably reported in magazines such as *Harper's*—the strikes and violence of the 1870's, the increasing (although never more than minute) presence of Marxian socialists and anarchists among the expanding foreign-born working population: all fed a growing sense of impending social cataclysm, a growing passion for law and order. Grim, fortresslike armories rose in American cities, and the National Guard was strengthened to deal with violence in the streets.

An attempt to limit the New York National Guard in 1881 and the continued strength of the Kearneyite movement in California served Nast as indices of the dread challenge to the social fabric posed by widespread forces of discontent (171, 172). Finally, a world-wide growth of anarchist violence culminated in the Haymarket explosion of May 1886 that killed seven Chicago policemen and led to the trial and sentencing to death of seven radical leaders. The worst imaginings of those who set themselves against the labor movement, of those who saw a threat to national unity in the unrest of the time, seemed to be realized. "Liberty is not anarchy," Nast intoned. The hand of Miss Liberty, clutching the accused Haymarket conspirators, bore a ring with the word "Union" emblazoned on it (173, 174).

What might be called a coalition of the "haves" took the lead in resisting new economic policies and criticizing labor unrest. It included those who stood to gain by hard money, low taxes, low wages, as well as intellectuals and reformers secure in their sense of the morality and the intellectual verity of their social outlook. But Nast does not fit readily into either group. He had no special ties to holders of large capital; and many genteel reformers had been Liberal Republicans and hence his political opponents. Rather, his insensitivity to the grievances that underlay the movements for soft money and a revived income tax, and the strikes and violence of the time, must be found in another source. Once again, we must look for the wellsprings of Nast's sentiment in his political ethics, and in the experience of the Civil War era that did so much to shape his social sensibility.

When Nast criticized with such passion the economic heresies of the late 'seventies and the early 'eighties, he was in fact giving voice to a shaken *élan* that appears increasingly in his artistic commentary, and that was shared by many of his contemporaries. The demand for new fiscal or tax policies, the strikes and riots were as one with the seeming decline of the Republican party into office-holding and ideological inconsequence; with the collapse of Radical Reconstruction and the other hopeful ventures of the Radical Republican era. Place-serving politicos, Greenbackers and silverites, labor organizers and violent social revolutionaries alike posed threats to the unified social order that the Civil War supposedly had created. They were a common danger to the triumphant, seamless Union of 1865; and had to be resisted with the same determination that secession, that other great threat to unity, to law and order, had been faced.

This explains why men with a large emotional stake in the Civil War reacted with such passion to the upsets of the 'seventies and the early 'eighties. John Hay, who had been Lincoln's private secretary, in 1883 published *The Bread Winners*, a novel filled with a fear of unions, strikes, and riots. Thomas Nast, too, could not let the demands and disturbances of a new—and different—time impinge on the vision of a unified people that was the great cause of his life.

Nast's commentary on international relations betrayed a similar loss of social confidence and optimism. His view of Europe became increasingly jaundiced and skeptical, particularly as the uplifting ventures in German and Italian unification of the 'sixties gave way to unadorned international power politics. Everywhere he noted—not without cause—the cynical application of power for selfish ends: in the designs of the European powers on the tottering Turkish empire (175); in the efforts of Marshal MacMahon, President of the Third Republic, to take on the mantle of Louis Napoleon (176, 177); in the aspirations of England and France for an Isthmian canal under European control (178).

Russia during the Civil War had been the great European friend of the embattled Union; under Alexander II her serfs were emancipated and other liberalizing reforms launched. But now opposition to the regime mounted, culminating in the assassination of Alexander in 1881, and an aggressive Pan-Slavism made the Russians a threat to the

West. The Russo-Turkish war that erupted in 1877 involved no principles, no causes: Nast saw it only as a macabre invitation to death (179, 180).

The artist's disillusionment extended to his own Fatherland. Once he had looked on Germany as the champion of liberal nationalism against the reactionary France of Louis Napoleon. By the early 1880's he was a sharp critic of Wilhelmine Germany's militarism, xenophobia, and anti-Semitism (181, 182).

At the same time, Nast's view of the United States's relationship to the outside world substantially changed. No longer did he dwell on the theme of America as the moral leader of an age of enlightenment, peace, and progress. Instead he saw his country existing in a hostile, Hobbesian world in which weakness was suicide (183). Economy-minded attempts to cut army appropriations threatened to leave the United States undefended and helpless. Guns, not ideas, defined the nation's bearing toward the world around it (184, 185).

Other aspects of American foreign policy disturbed him. He bracketed German-Americans with Irish-Americans as hyphenates improperly continuing to champion their homelands (186). Attempts to sell American securities to British investors while an inflationary greenback currency existed smacked of international dishonesty (187). When James G. Blaine became Secretary of State in 1881, Nast feared that this politico would destroy the fragile structure of good relations with other countries created by his less flamboyant predecessor Frederick T. Frelinghuysen (188).

The American view of foreign affairs underwent a profound change in the 'seventies. Emphasis on the causes of liberty, progress, and republicanism gave way to more overtly materialistic ends; the expansion of American capital and commerce now seemed more important than the expansion of American ideals. A good measure of this alteration is the circular that Secretary of State William M. Evarts sent to his diplomatic officers in July 1877. "It is believed that the period has now arrived," Evarts announced, "when it would be wise for all the nations . . . to consider more carefully than heretofore how they may best enlarge their trade with each other." The principal political benefits to be gained were "stability, peace, law, and order"; "popular energy" would be turned from "revolution or military aggrandizement" to "more peaceful and profitable enterprises." The blessings of economic profit and social stability had taken precedence over the ideal of the Great Republic setting an example to the world.

January 19, 1878

"Ideal Money."

"Universal Suffrage can, if it likes, repudiate the whole debt; it can, if it likes, decree
soft-soap to be currency." *The Louisville Courier-Journal*

July 31, 1875

Iron and Blood—This "Don't Scare Worth a Cent."

April 11, 1874

The Cradle of Liberty in Danger.

"Fee-Fi-Fo-Fum!" The genie of Massachusetts smells blue blood.

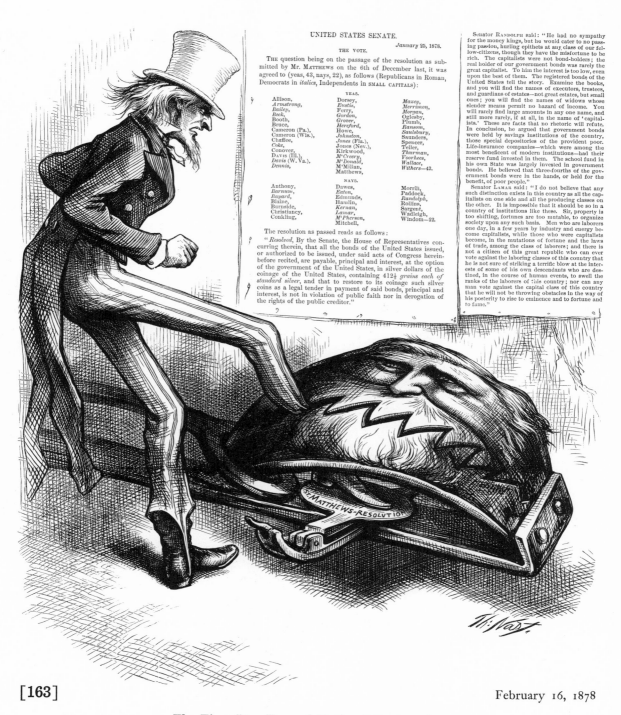

February 16, 1878

The First Step Toward National Bankruptcy.

AS A VERY IMPORTANT SOURCE OF STRENGTH AND SECURITY, CHERISH
PUBLIC CREDIT. G.W.

BUT BY VIGOROUS EXERTIONS IN TIME OF PEACE TO DISCHARGE THE DEBTS WHICH
MAY HAVE OCCASIONED, NOT UNGENEROUSLY THROWING UPON POSTERITY THE
BURTHEN WHICH WE OUR-
SELVES OUGHT TO BEAR."
G. WASHINGTON.
(FAREWELL ADDRESS.)

"WE OUGHT TO PLACE THE PUBLIC CREDIT ON GROUNDS
WHICH CANNOT BE DISTURBED AND TO PREVENT THAT PROGRESSIVE ACCUMULATION
OF DEBT WHICH MUST ULTIMATELY ENDANGER ALL GOVERNMENTS."
G.W.

THE
PUBLIC CREDIT
IS A MATTER
OF HIGH
IMPORTANCE
TO THE
NATIONAL
HONOR AND
PROSPERITY."
G.W.

IN GOD WE TRUST.

90 CENTS

STATE DEBT
COUNTY DEBT
NATIONAL DEBT
CITY DEBT
PRIVATE
PLURIBUS UNUM
UNION OF DEBTS

LABOR AGAINST CAPITAL
REDUCING THE U.S.

The Two Georges.

GEORGE III. TO GEORGE WASHINGTON. "I say, George—Daddy—is that the free and enlightened cherub for whom you fought? Don't you think you had better write another Farewell Address to him?"

March 23, 1878

[164]

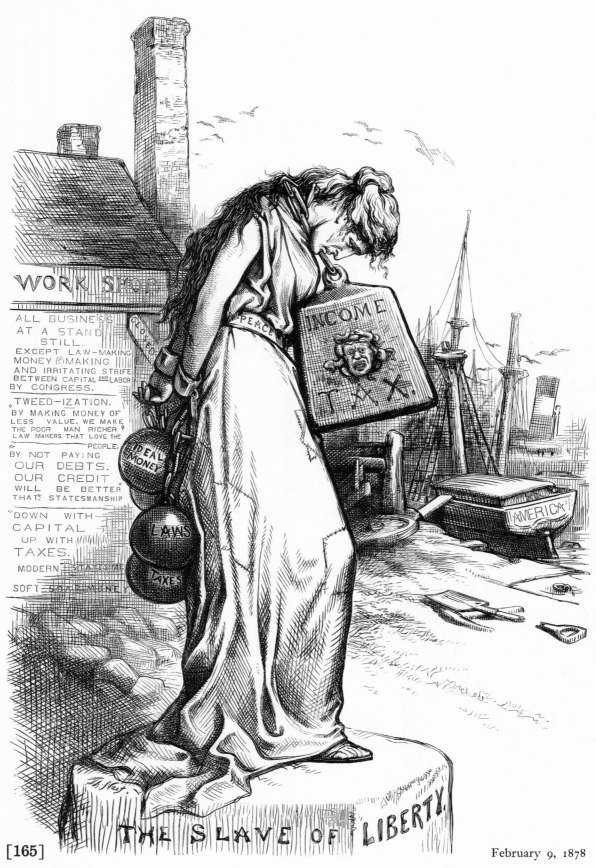

February 9, 1878

Peace with a **War** Measure.

March 2, 1878

Will He Dare Do It?

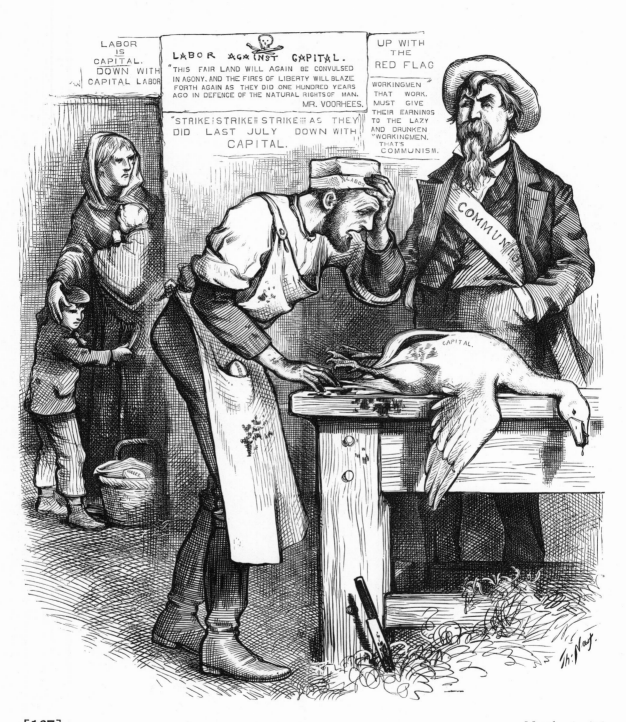

March 16, 1878

Always Killing the Goose That Lays the Golden Egg.

COMMUNISTIC STATESMAN (*without responsibility*). "Nothing in it, after all; it's too bad; now I thought he was just full of them."

June 1, 1878

The "Internationalists" Are To Make
the World All One Millennium—(Chaos).

June 22, 1878

"Home, Sweet Home! There's No Place Like Home!"

DESTROYER OF ALL. "Home ties are nothing. Family ties are nothing. Every thing that is—is nothing."

April 5, 1879

Hatching.

How much longer will birds of prey be allowed to gorge themselves on the savings
of the self-denying and industrious—and escape the consequences?

May 7, 1881

"New York Must Go—Down."

SCUM. "When this law is passed, you will be so disorganized that you will not be able to muster a corporal's guard against me."

April 10, 1880

Social Science Solved.

THE MODERN ARCHIMEDES. *"Eureka! Eureka!"*
"Constant Vigilance" (committee) "is the price of liberty" in San Francisco.

February 7, 1885

Liberty Is Not Anarchy.

September 4, 1886

Dynamite and Panic in the Air!

June 30, 1877

Peace Rumors.

LET US HAVE (A) PEACE (PIECE). [*The Turk wishes he was a Christian.*]

[176]   June 16, 1877

On a Bust Again.

Vive-la—.

[177]   July 14, 1877

The Marshal Trying It On.

This is not the first time it has *dis-* and *ex-*tinguished the
head of France.

[178]

March 13, 1880

The European Plan.

February 2, 1878

Into the Jaws of Death.

June 29, 1878

Halt, Cossack!—So Far, but No Farther!

[181]   January 22, 1881

"Das Deutsche Vaterland" Is Above Criticism

FROTH. "I will cut you into small pieces if you say dem mean tings again!"

London, Jan. 3.—A Berlin correspondent telegraphs as follows: "Reports received here of a demonstration in the United States with the object of protesting against the Anti-Jewish agitation here is producing a very unfavorable impression, the feeling being that Germany can tolerate no intervention in home affairs by a foreign State."

[182]   February 13, 1886

The Difference Between Vater Land and Mother Country.

May 19, 1877

The Advanced Age.

MERCURY. "What under the sun are you doing?"
MARS. "Mortals will make *such* big guns, and this is the consequence."

[184]

Peace Insecure—Afraid for Her Life.

February 13, 1875

Peace Secure—Safe and Protected.

UNCLE SAM'S ANDERSONVILLE
FOR HIS SERVANTS
ABROAD
AND AT HOME.

POLITICAL "CAPITAL."

Whereas, Uncle Sam's *honest* servants can hardly keep body and soul together on their present salary,

Resolved, That we present this "economical" bill to reduce their salaries further, so that they may be compelled to steal, and keep their fellow "statesmen" (*à la* TWEED) in countenance.

[185]

February 26, 1876

Republican "Simplicity."

April 14, 1877

Reform Is Necessary in the Foreign Line.

U. S. (*like an uncle*). "If you come *simply as Americans*, this is the place. But if you persist in your distinct nationality, you must call at the State Department, where all foreign affairs are considered."

August 19, 1876

A Financial Lesson.

"An Eagle stayed his flight, and entreated a Lion to make an alliance with him to their mutual advantage. The Lion replied: 'I have no objection, but you must excuse me for requiring you to find surety for your good faith; for how can I trust any one as a friend who is able to fly away from his bargain whenever he pleases?"—Aesop.

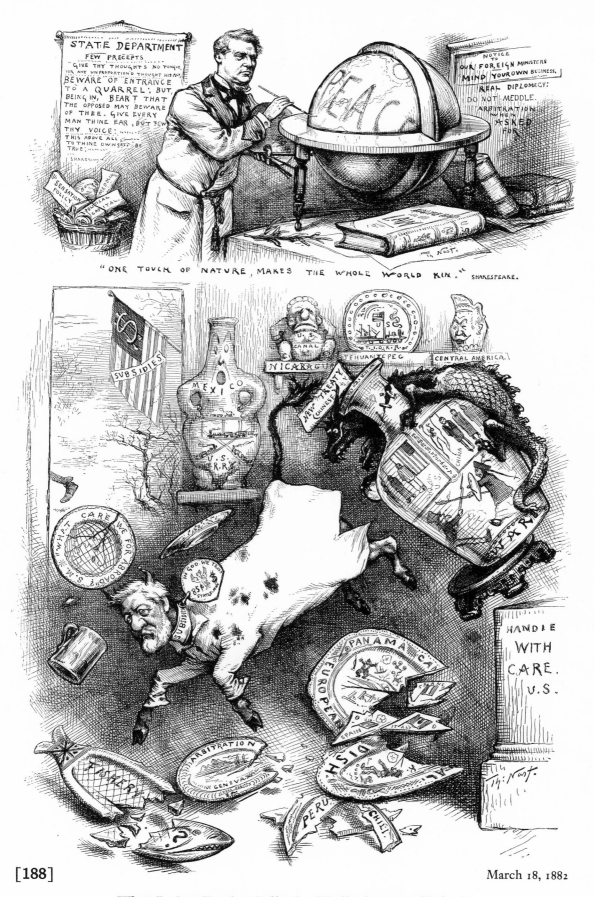

March 18, 1882

What Is Our Foreign Policy?—(Frelinghuysen—Blaine.)

XI
The Passing of
Political Radicalism

In the wake of the 1872 Republican triumph, Nast wryly caricatured himself: "Our Artist's Occupation Gone" (189). His offhand sketch foretold the coming predicament of the artist of Radical Republicanism. For the next decade and more he would have to cope with a steady decline in the political fortunes of his party, and with the diminishing vitality of his Radical Republican beliefs. Nast commented on this transformation with his customary brilliance. But ultimately he had to face the fact that the new political order was not one to which he could speak with artistry and force.

Grant's second term of office did not still the discontent of many Republicans with their party. The New York diarist George Templeton Strong observed in 1873: "There seems to be a prevalent feeling that a new party is wanted. Republicanism has grown immoral in its old age and survived much of its usefulness." Much was made of the President's supposed ambition for a third term—his "Caesarism"—and of his use of Federal troops to protect Southern Negro voters. Editor George W. Curtis of *Harper's* continued to differ with Nast over the government's southern policy. He told the artist: "My feeling is that the country feels that there has been rather too much bayonet."

Horace Greeley died soon after his defeat in 1872; but his successor as editor of the *Tribune*, Whitelaw Reid, continued to criticize the administration. He was joined by the flamboyant James Gordon Bennett, Jr., publisher of the New York *Herald*, and by many other journals with Democratic and Liberal Republican opinions.

Nast as a Republican partisan reacted strongly to the journalistic attack on Grant; no one knew better what influence important publicists could wield (190). Reid's criticism especially disturbed him. The *Tribune*, after all, had been the great national newspaper of the Republican party in the period of the Civil War (191). He treated the eccentric Bennett with a lighter touch. In 1874 the *Herald* threw New York City into turmoil by trumpeting the story that the animals in the Central Park Zoo had escaped. Nast utilized the incident to ridicule the view that Grant was given over to dictatorial ambitions and rule by bayonet (192).

But the harsh fact of corruption in the second Grant administration could not readily be ignored. Nast was forced to confront not a moral failure on Grant's part, or a sudden lapse in the ethical standard of the government, but something even more distressing. The sorry scandals of the time were so many fever spots on a body politic that was undergoing a profound change of purpose and tone. No less than the enormities of the Tweed Ring, the corruption of the Grant administration was part of the price paid for the replacement of a politics of ideology by a politics of organization. Nast had the unhappy duty of commenting on these ugly aspects of a political transformation to which he was profoundly opposed—a change going on within a party to which he was profoundly committed.

In May 1874 Secretary of the Treasury William A. Richardson came under fire for granting a lucrative contract for the collection of unpaid Federal taxes to John D. Sanborn, an associate of Ben Butler. Scathingly, Nast advised the recreant Richardson to resign—as indeed the Secretary soon did (193). This was only one of a series of embarrassments for the administration; but Grant stood by his associates as trouble descended on them. He appointed Richardson to the Court of Claims.

Soon after he sought Senate confirmation of Alexander R. Shepherd as governor of the newly created territorial District of Columbia. Shepherd had been Washington's public works commissioner—and political boss—in the early 1870's. He was chiefly responsible for the paving, lighting, and other improvements that turned the capital from a slovenly town into a respectable city; and in his time Washington's Negroes made important—if impermanent—gains in their civil and social rights. But bribes and corrupt contracts figured prominently in Shepherd's rule. A Senate self-righteously indignant over Shepherd's public morals—and self-interestedly jealous of his political skill and power—rejected the nomination. Grant's loyalty, which a few years before might have struck Nast as a measure of his hero's humanity, now was unpleasant evidence of a general decline in political morality. His comment on the affair was the only cartoon critical of Grant that he ever drew (194).

No less disturbing was the behavior of Secretary of War William W. Belknap. His particular dereliction was to have sold post trader-ships in Indian territory—a perversion of Grant's hopeful Indian policy of peace and assimilation. That the wrongdoing was by the civilian head of the Army of the Union heightened Nast's indignation. He condemned Belknap with a cartoon imagery that a few years before had been reserved for the Tweed Ring (195).

If these instances of corruption were one measure of the Radical Republican political style gone sour, the changing status of Radical Reconstruction was another. Nast commented with a new asperity on the misbehavior of Negro members of the South Carolina legislature, and on the maladministration of the state's Republican governor, Franklin J. Moses (196, 197).

As distressing as the loss of Republican purity was the decline of Republican power. The Democrats won a majority of the House of Representatives in 1874, their first national triumph since prewar days. Republican leaders speculated gloomily on the significance of this event. James A. Garfield called the Democratic victory "part of a great reaction in the public mind from the war, its causes and incidents. . . . A spirit of unrest and unfixed suspicion and distrust has taken possession of the public mind." The Democrats maintained control of the lower chamber for the remainder of the decade, in 1878 gained temporary control of the Senate, and in 1876 won a popular majority of the Presidential vote.

Nast commented brilliantly on the new and precarious position of the Grand Old Party. During the 1874 campaign—that first blow to Republican hegemony—he introduced the figure of the Republican elephant. At first labeled "the Republican vote," his was a cumbersome, purposeless beast: in effect, what Nast feared his party had become (198, 199). Just three years before he had given his audience the terrible, ideologically charged image of the Tammany tiger—a symbol which served him too as a representation of the ravenous Democratic party. Now with equal prescience he caught the transformation of a politics of ideological confrontation into a politics of competing placemen.

The Democratic party remained for him what it had been for a decade: a collection of skeletal figures from the unlamented political past, of shabby and suspect organizations such as Tammany Hall and the slightly more respectable Manhattan Club (200, 201). Uneasily Nast confronted the novelty of a Democratic House of Representatives after the 1874 electoral disaster. He took comfort in the fact that the Presidency and the Senate were still Republican (202). But he had little faith in the ability of Democratic Congressional leaders Samuel S. Cox and Fernando Wood to set the party on a new course by stressing reform and downplaying the issues of the Civil War era (203). His skepticism was justified. Democratic attempts to establish a strong and unified Congressional stance ran afoul of factional differences, and party spokesmen devoted themselves to rhetorical reprises of the old issues (204, 205).

In truth, the effectiveness of both parties declined during the 1870's. Hard times, which might have been expected to increase their unity, only heightened their ideological diffusion. Time and again on the central issue of the currency huge bipartisan majorities took a position —and then quickly reversed themselves. Consistency and the ability to effect policy were casualties of the change from a politics shaped by ideology to one shaped by organization. It was not until the following decade that party unity and cohesion would reappear.

Nast recorded these changes—but he also resisted them. He could not ignore the moral lapses of the Grant administration; but he had an eye too for the hypocrisies of its attackers. He paid his respects to Congressional critics whose public morals were little better than those they attacked, or who advocated reductions in government salaries while they condemned corruption in the civil service (206, 207). He recognized that the Democratic stress on retrenchment in the armed services had the purpose of reducing further the already weak Federal presence in the South (208).

Most of all Nast retained his special feeling for Grant as the savior of the Union. During the administration's last unhappy years he saw the President as a man unjustly burdened with the woes of a nation— and a party—fallen on hard times (209, 210). When Grant left the Presidency in March 1877, the artist commented in an elegaic tone full of the sense that an era had passed (211).

The Passing of Political Radicalism

The transformation of American politics to which Nast bore uneasy witness came to a climax with the election of 1876. This was the last Presidential campaign in which the issues and emotions of Civil War and Reconstruction figured prominently; the first in which the interests and viewpoints of the new political order determined the result.

Nast contributed to the 1876 campaign his by now familiar indictment of the opposition. Although the Democratic candidate, New York Governor Samuel J. Tilden, owned a newly earned reputation as a reformer, he had been long a power in the state's Tammany-ridden organization. Nast harped on this and on what he took to be Tilden's equivocal position during the Civil War (212, 213). He conjured up a Democratic menagerie: a two-headed tiger made up of the hard-money Tilden and his soft-money running mate Thomas A. Hendricks; the gaunt and hungry wolves of the Solid South and the patronage-starved organization (214, 215, 216). He paid special attention to the continued, violent repression of Southern Negroes. A massacre of Negro militiamen in Hamburg, South Carolina, allowed him once again to evoke for his audience the specter of a violent, unregenerate—and Democratic—white South (217, 218).

But the old issues no longer had the power that once was theirs. Tilden won a majority of the popular vote—and, it seemed at first, an electoral victory as well. But the electoral returns of South Carolina, Louisiana, and Florida were contested, and the election entered a legal and political crisis that did not end until the eve of the inauguration of a new President in March 1877. Complex negotiations produced an ajudicating electoral commission, and then Democratic acceptance of the commission's decision in favor of the Hayes electors.

The months of tension before the final compromise—the mounting intransigence of Tilden's supporters, the overhanging threat of violence as Democratic governors and editors spoke of using troops to ensure Tilden's election—was unpleasantly reminiscent of the eve of the Civil War (219). But the time, the issues—the political environment—were different. Militancy gave way to backstairs negotiation; this generation of political leaders was too close to the tragedy of the 1860's readily to re-enact it. Leaders in both sections and of both parties found their way to compromise. Interests were traded off: Southern desires for public and private investment in railroads and other forms of economic development; Northern readiness to give up the faltering effort to enforce Negro civil rights. The passions of Henry Watterson of the Louisville *Courier-Journal* belonged to an earlier political time; the current note was struck by mediating editors such as the Cincinnati *Commercial*'s Murat Halstead (220). Publicists, politicians, and businessmen of both parties—the shapers of a new, post-ideological American politics—worked out the necessary compromise, and Hayes was peacefully inaugurated.

But peace had its price. The battered GOP that emerged from the crisis bore little resemblance to the party of the wartime and postwar years (221). Domestic tranquility had been bought at the cost of the Radical Republican ethos.

[189] November 23, 1872

Our Artist's Occupation Gone.

Th. Nast. "It's all very funny to you; but what am I to do now?"

Diogenes Still Looking.—

"We are the gentlemen you are in search of."

April 15, 1876

[191]

February 28, 1874

The New York Tribune's "Disclosures."

OTHELLO (*Uncle Sam*). "Villain, be sure of it; give me the ocular proof;
Or, by the worth of mine eternal soul,
Thou hadst been better have been born a dog,
Than answer my wak'd wrath."
IAGO ("*Professor*" *of Scandal*). "Is it come to this?"
OTHELLO. "Make me to see it; or (at the least) so prove it,
That the probation bear no hinge, nor loop,
To hang a doubt on: or, woe upon thy life!
If thou dost slander her, and torture me,
Never pray more: abandon all remorse;
On horror's head horrors accumulate:
Do deeds to make heaven weep, all earth amaz'd,
For nothing canst thou to damnation add,
Greater than that."—SHAKSPEARE.

February 6, 1875

The Biggest Scare and Hoax Yet!—The Wild Animals Let Loose
Again by the Zoomorphism Press.

[193]

May 23, 1874

"The Next Thing in Order."

(The portrait of the Secretary of the Treasury is drawn as mildly as possible.)

July 18, 1874

"Don't Let Us Have any More of This Nonsense. It Is a Good Trait
To Stand by One's Friends; but—"

**It Struck (in Blowing Over).—Picking Even the Poor Soldiers' Bones
To Feather Their Nest.**

[196]

March 14, 1874

Colored Rule in a Reconstructed (?) State.

(THE MEMBERS CALL EACH OTHER THIEVES, LIARS, RASCALS, AND COWARDS.)

COLUMBIA. "You are aping the lowest whites. If you disgrace your race in this way you had better take back seats."

September 26, 1874

The Commandments in South Carolina.

"We've pretty well smashed that; but I suppose, Massa MOSES, you can get another one."

The Third-Term Panic.

"An Ass, having put on the Lion's skin, roamed about in the forest, and amused himself by frightening all the foolish animals he met with in his wanderings."—SHAKSPEARE or BACON.

November 21, 1874

Caught in a Trap—The Result of the Third-Term Hoax.

June 13, 1874

A Dead Failure.

"A gathering of the dead . . . a kind of love-feast among some ancient skeletons from the grave-yard of the ancient Bourbon party. . . . The assembled skeletons shook one another's bony hands, smiled as skeletons are wont to do, and rattled their old bones in forced gleefulness over the drawn battles in New Hampshire and Connecticut, which it pleased them to call Democratic victories!"—*Chicago Times* (Democratic).

December 12, 1874

The Rising of the Dead.

TAMMANY SKELETON. "How long shall we be allowed to stay above-ground?"
MANHATTAN SKELETON. "It's only a ticket of leave, and you—I mean we—must be on our good behavior, as we are only on trial."

December 5, 1874

Now Gnaw Away!

December 11, 1875

"Ay, There's the Rub!"

"Take off those stripes, and it will look like a lamb."

February 5, 1876

"Amnesty"; or, The End of the Peaceful
(Democratic) Tiger.

February 26, 1876

No Rudder—No Aim.

It is not so easy to catch that dear little (Republican) lamb, after all.

April 15, 1876

The Political Problem.

The law-maker and law-breaker—one and inseparable.

CIVIL SERVICE REFORM.

IF YOU WANT GOOD WATCH-DOGS, YOU MUST PAY A GOOD PRICE FOR THEM, AND KEEP THEM WELL.

A HUNGRY DOG WILL STEAL.

IF YOU FIND ANY HONEST, CAPABLE, AND FAITHFUL TO YOUR INTERESTS, DON'T TURN THEM OUT TO STARVE WHEN THEY ARE TOO OLD TO WORK.

THE PRESENT SYSTEM WILL ONLY PRODUCE CURS.

[207]

April 22, 1876

Cur-Tail-Phobia.

U. S. "Because he steals? You are, as usual, 'Mr. Statesman,' at the wrong end."

May 30, 1874

"There Is Nothing Mean About Us."

UNCLE SAM. "What Congress proposes to reduce our Army and Navy to!"

October 24, 1874

A Burden He Has To Shoulder.

And they say, "He wants a third term."

May 13, 1876

The Crowning Insult to Him Who Occupies the Presidential Chair.

[210]

EXTINCTUS AMABITUR IDEM. — EX MORE.

Ulysses. Time hath...a wallet at his back,
Wherein he puts alms for oblivion,
A great-sized monster of ingratitudes:
Those scraps are good deeds past: which are devour'd
As fast as they are made, forgot as soon
As done: Perseve'rance....
Keeps honor bright: To have done, is to hang
Quite out of fashion, like a rusty nail
In monumental mockery. Take the instant way;
For honor travels in a strait so narrow
Where one but goes abreast: keep then the path;
For emulation hath a thousand sons,
That one by one pursue: If you give way,
Or hedge aside from the direct forthright,
Like to an enter'd tide, they all rush by,
And leave you hindmost;—
Or, like a gallant horse fallen in first rank,
Lie there for pavement to the abject rear,
O'errun and trampled on: Then, what they do in present,
Though less than yours in past, must o'ertop yours:
For time is like a fashionable host,
That slightly shakes his parting guest by the hand;
And with his arms outstretch'd, as he would fly,
Grasps in the comer: Welcome ever smiles,
And farewell goes out sighing. O, let not virtue seek
Remuneration for the thing it was;
For beauty, wit,
High birth, vigor of bone, desert in service,
Love, friendship, charity, are subjects all
To envious and calumniating time.
One touch of nature makes the whole world kin,—
That all, with one consent, praise new-born gawds,
Though they are made and moulded of things past:
And give to dust, that is a little gilt,
More laud than gilt o'er-dusted.—SHAKSPEARE.

Functus Officio.

March 17, 1877

[211]

The following text appears within the illustration:

THIS "MACHINE" HAS PUT OUT MANY A FIRE.

REPUBLICAN "MACHINE" 1861 TO —

"WE WANT TO GO BACK." THE CRY OF THE OUTS.

"THE PARTY NOW IN (POWER) WILL BE OUT, (1877) AND THE ANCIENT DEMOCRACY WITH ITS HONEST PRINCIPLES OF ADMINISTRATION WILL COME AGAIN INTO POWER." KERNAN.

WHITE HOUSE. WASHINGTON D.C.

"TO THE VICTORS BELONG THE SPOILS." A. JACKSON.

TIGER AMERICUS.

"PURITY. ECONOMY. AND HONESTY THAT WAS TAUGHT BY ITS FOUNDERS." KERNAN.

"IDIOTS OR KNAVES." SAY THIS IS A MACHINE.

N.Y. DEMOCRATIC PARTY. SAM TILDEN

TAMMANY

THIS IS A GONFALON

THIS IS NOT A "MACHINE." "IT IS THE 'SPIRIT OF REFORM' THE SIMPLE VIRTUES, PRINCIPLES OF HONESTY, AND THE WISDOM OF OUR FATHERS, WHICH THE DEMOCRATIC PARTY HAS EVER UPHELD." H. SEYMOUR.

[212]

May 20, 1876

"The Foremost Champion of This Spirit of Reform."—H. Seymour.

He will *run* the "machine" (raised "out of the gutter") to St. Louis "as a unit," then to the "White House," and the people who doubt it are "idiots or knaves."

[213]

Between Two Fires.

Soldiers. *"Whose side were you on?"*
Reformed Usufruct. *"I—I was—busy in court with a Railroad Case."*

October 14, 1876

July 22, 1876

The Democratic (Deformed) Tiger "Fixed."

REFORMED "GAMBLER STATESMAN." "I'll bet $10,000 that this is the greatest de-
formed (*reformed*, I mean) animal going; $10,000 that it is going to lick every thing
else in the field; $10,000 that this double-headed, double-faced tiger can be turned
any way to gull the American People; $10,000 that nobody could tell *now* that he
had ever lost his head or his tail."

[215]

October 21, 1876

"The Solid South"—Gaunt and Hungry.

U.S. TREASURY.
THIS IS THE DEMOCRATIC WOLF GAUNT AND HUNGRY.
RAG BABY
Th. Nast.

[216]

November 25, 1876

Waiting.

The "Bloody Shirt" Reformed.

GOVERNOR TILDEN. "It is not I, but the idea of reform which I represent."

August 12, 1876

[217]

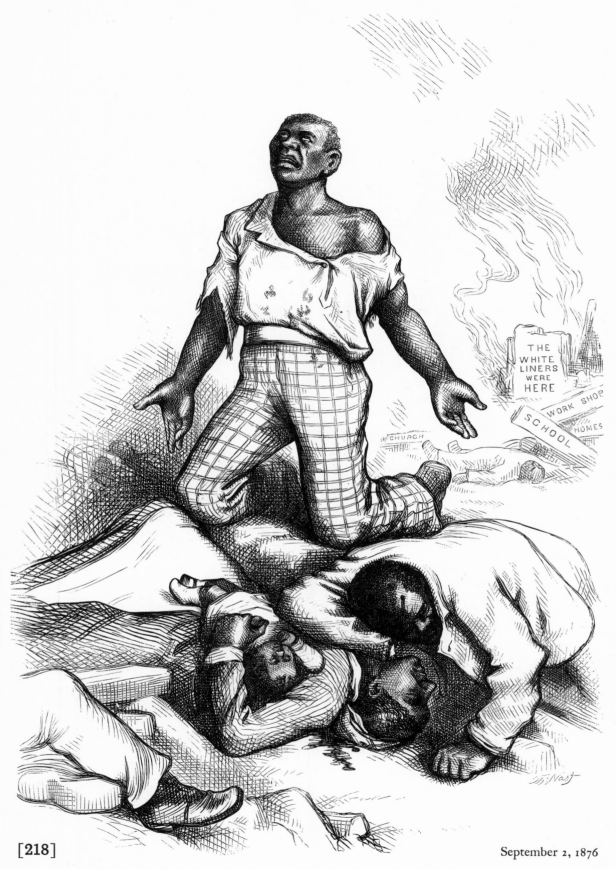

September 2, 1876

"Is <u>This</u> a Republican Form of Government? Is <u>This</u> Protecting Life, Liberty, or Property? Is <u>This</u> the Equal Protection of the Laws?"

MR. LAMAR (*Democrat, Mississippi*). "In the words of the inspired poet, 'Thy gentleness has made thee great.'" [Did Mr. LAMAR mean the colored race?]

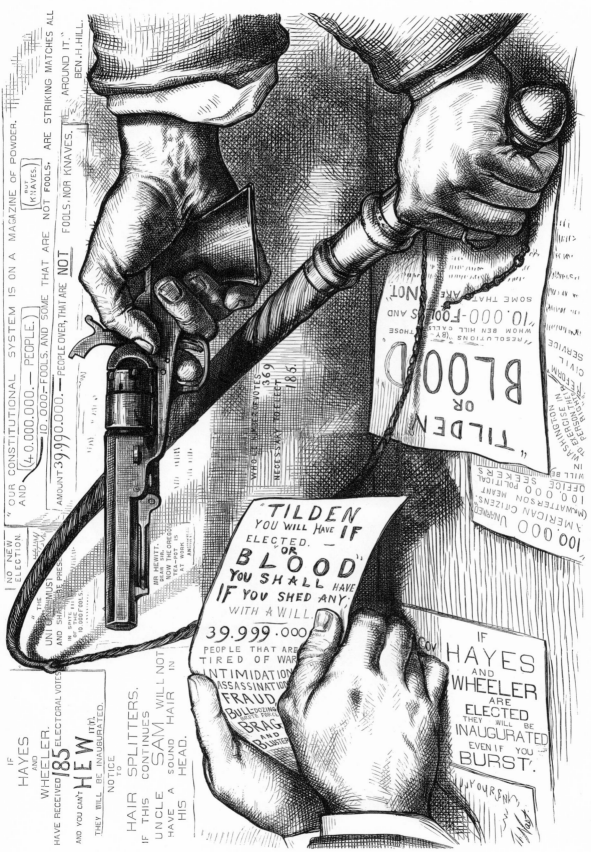

January 27, 1877

Compromise—Indeed!

[219]

February 3, 1877

Fire and Water Make Vapor.

What a cooling off will be there, my countrymen!

March 24, 1877

"Another Such Victory, and I am Undone."—Pyrrhus.

XII

The Transformation of American Politics

By the end of the 1870's a new American political style prevailed, in which the issues and attitudes of the Civil War and Reconstruction were only a dim memory. The ideological and aesthetic problems that this new milieu posed for Thomas Nast ultimately proved to be insurmountable. As his relationship to the political order became less and less satisfactory, so declined his ability to speak to his audience. His work drew its form and vigor from the concerns of the Civil War, of Radical Republicanism. When these faded, so did his influence and his art.

The inauguration of Rutherford B. Hayes in March 1877 dramatized the change in political periods. The new President's quick removal of the remaining Federal troops in the South ended any hope of meaningful Negro participation in American political life. And it signified the readiness of the two parties to disengage themselves from the passions, the issues of the Civil War and postwar years. Although Republicans would continue to wave the Bloody Shirt, and Southerners to champion the Lost Cause, their commitments would be little more than symbolic and rhetorical.

With Grant's departure from the Presidency, Nast's strongest link to national Republican politics was gone. Henceforward his reaction to political issues was increasingly aloof and dispassionate—a tone markedly different from the commitment that had informed his art before. He remained one of the major voices of Republicanism; but he had scant sympathy for Hayes's personality or policies. From July to November of 1877 Nast devoted himself to cartoons on non-political matters because of his disagreement with the editor and publisher of *Harper's* over the new President's Southern policy. His relations with George W. Curtis, never idyllic, were strained further when Roscoe Conkling referred to Curtis as the editor of "that journal made famous by the pencil of Thomas Nast."

The continued threat of Democratic supremacy was the glue that held differing Republicans together. The GOP suffered grievous losses in the local elections of 1877; and in 1878 the Democrats took both branches of Congress for the first time since 1856 (222). Nast gloomily contemplated a Democratic party hungry for spoils and threatening to reimburse Southerners for their wartime losses (223, 224).

But it was hard to sustain the old sense of Democratic sinfulness and Republican virtue. In 1879 Nast drew the first cartoon in which the Republican elephant and the Democratic donkey appeared together as the symbols of the new party system. No discernible ideological differences distinguished these valueless, neuter beasts: a torpid GOP threatened by Senator John Sherman's equivocation on specie resumption was hardly the moral superior of a Democracy that might yet respond to hard-money advocate Thomas Bayard (225).

The election of 1880 was the first important milestone in the decline of Nast's political commitment—and his artistic vigor. He had a special distaste for the leading Republican contender, James G. Blaine (226). Blaine embodied better than any other politician of his generation the transformation of the Republican party—and of American politics—from the social and ideological commitments of the Civil War era to the blander organizational style of the Gilded Age. But James A. Garfield, the party's final choice, no more captured Nast's imagination than had Hayes four years before.

Nast satirized Tilden's hope (as it proved, unfounded) that the lightning of a Presidential nomination might strike again (227). And he brushed aside the Greenback party candidacy of James B. Weaver (228). But the Democratic nominee, Winfield Scott Hancock, had been a Union war hero and had not been a party to the political battles of the postwar years. For the first time since the Civil War a Democratic candidate escaped Nast's instinct for the jugular. He contented himself with mild portrayals of Hancock as a Gulliver beset by party Lilliputians and Brobdingnagians (229, 230).

The political developments that followed the election of Garfield only deepened Nast's conviction that both parties were in a state of decay. The elaborate struggle between Blaine and Conkling for party supremacy was only another measure of a political system increasingly devoid of meaning (231). There was a grim propriety to the fact that Garfield was assassinated in July 1881 by an insane office-seeker who identified himself with the stalwart party faction of Vice President Chester Arthur. The cause of the Confederacy justified assassination to a disordered mind fifteen years before; now the quest for patronage and intraparty factional strife served equally well. The generational change was complete: a politics of organization now occupied the place in the American public order that once had belonged to a politics of sectional and social ideology.

Nast had little rapport with the terms and style of the new politics. He was repelled by the trial of Garfield's killer, Charles Guiteau, which dwelt on the more outlandish aspects of the assassin's insanity (232). (It is suggestive that the eulogy of Garfield that most moved contemporaries was delivered by James G. Blaine—the Republican whom Nast most disliked.) In the past he had looked on politics as the most important of social functions: the highroad to progress and reform. But now Congress and the politicians by their very existence threatened the well-being of capital, of labor, of the people (233, 234). "Citizen Beaver and 'Statesman' Sloth" confronted each other as antagonistic, incompatible social types (235).

Nast's attitude was far from unique. But most of the influential spokesmen in American life who shared it came to their disillusion earlier and more easily. And Nast's distress was in a way purer, less self-interested. Unlike editors such as George Curtis and E.L. Godkin, or would-be men of influence like Henry Adams, he was not threatened by the new political order; no ambitions of his had been thwarted or frustrated. He was still the great popular artistic spokesman of Republicanism; he was much sought after by political leaders, even those he lampooned. Nast's unease came only from his sense that a great cause—the cause of Radical Republicanism—had gone awry.

His stricken political sensibilities would lead him finally to the ultimate step of party disaffection. Grover Cleveland, who rose rapidly as a Governor of New York at odds with the politics of both parties, had attractions for Nast sufficient to override the stigma of a Democratic label. He looked favorably on Cleveland as Governor and then as a Presidential candidate—against Blaine—although he had his doubts as to Cleveland's ability to handle the spoilsmen of his own party (236, 237). That Nast—and *Harper's Weekly*—should support a Democratic candidate for President deeply shocked the magazine's Republican audience. A flood of aggrieved or angry letters revealed how strong still were the popular wellsprings of Republicanism.

But even Cleveland's narrow victory in 1884 had little impact on Nast's changed view of American politics. He remained detached from a time of new issues and a new political style. Once his art had been governed by an overriding sense of the moral and ideological distinction between the parties. Now the politician using the arts of patronage, intimidation, and demagoguery belonged with fine impartiality to both the GOP and the Democracy (238, 239). Nast's great Tweedian vulture—squat, loathsome—appeared once more: this time to represent the political system at large (240).

In August 1885 Thomas Nast mourned the death of Ulysses S. Grant (241). In truth he commemorated more than the passing of "The Hero of Our Age." His was a threnody for the political era, now gone, that had breathed life and power into his art.

Nast's career in effect was over. He left *Harper's* in 1886; but he and his magazine had started on divergent paths years before. Fletcher Harper, the creator and publisher of *Harper's Weekly* and Nast's staunch supporter, died in May 1877. The new publisher, Joseph W. Harper, Jr., shared editor George Curtis's view of public issues. What was more, he led the magazine away from its political emphasis toward topics better suited to an audience increasingly feminine, decreasingly caught up in political issues. (It is suggestive of the declining public involvement in party politics that political figures begin to be labeled in *Harper's* cartoons in the early 1880's.) A new magazine and a new artist came to the forefront of political commentary. The comic magazine *Puck* first appeared in March 1877, and its chief political cartoonist, Joseph Keppler, came to dominate the genre in America. Both magazine and artist were observers of a political ambience that amused more than moved them. They treated politics as a national pastime rather than the serious instrument of national self-improvement that it had been for Nast and *Harper's* during the great days of Radical Republicanism.

Nast's art, too, underwent a sea change in this time of political transformation. Photochemical reproduction replaced engraved woodblocks around 1880. Thereafter he drew with a pen not a pencil, and on paper instead of a wooden block. The result was a harder, sparser line to his drawings, unsparing of deficiencies of technique that had been obscured by the softer medium of block engraving. The change only underscored the fact that Nast had less and less to say: that his artistic force and imagination had declined in step with his political commitment and interest.

Nast's final years were dogged by financial as well as artistic insufficiency. He lost considerable money in the Grant & Ward investment brokerage, whose failure wiped out Ulysses Grant's savings. He did free-lance work for a variety of magazines; in 1888 contracted with the Democratic National Committee to prepare pro-Cleveland cartoons; in 1892 established the short-lived *Nast's Weekly* and received some Republican campaign money. By the turn of the century he was down on his luck. In March 1902 Secretary of State John Hay, an old admirer, induced President Theodore Roosevelt to give Nast the consular post in Guayaquil, Ecuador. The artist accepted this final, meager gift of the party for whom he had done so much. But after barely six months of residence, on December 7, 1902, he died of yellow fever.

Harper's Weekly noted at the time: "He belongs so much to the past that the impression has naturally spread that he is an old man." In fact, Nast was 62. His art had belonged to a brief, distinctive era, by the turn of the century only a faint (and distasteful) memory. Not until our own time would Nast's drawings recover their original evocative power.

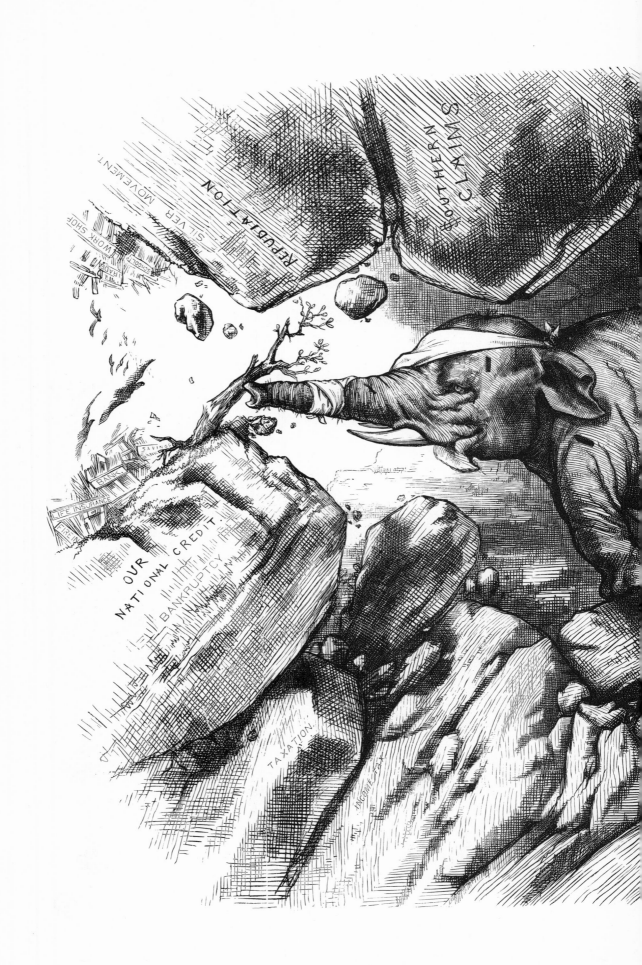

Stand From Under!

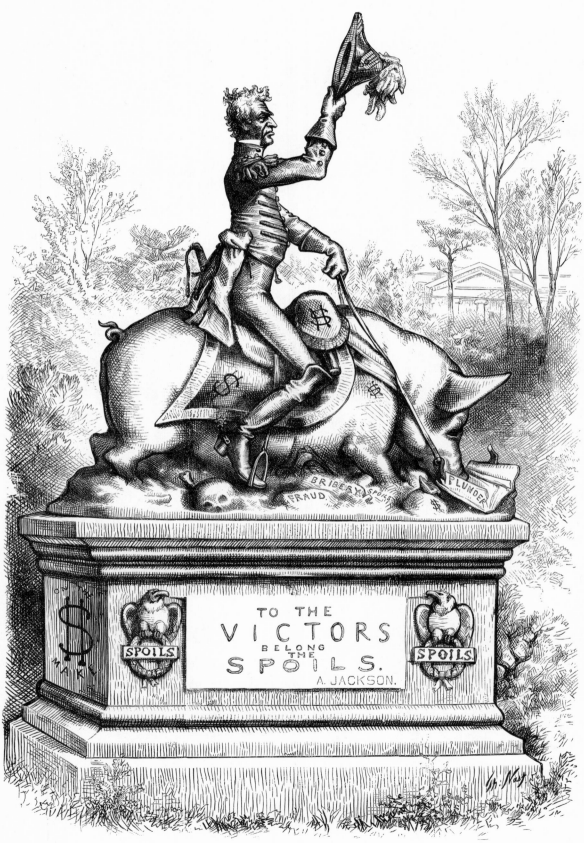

April 28, 1877

In Memoriam—Our Civil Service as It Was.

May 4, 1878

Probabilities.

WASHINGTON.—Frequent southerly breezes, occasionally growing stronger, and at times threatening to become a perfect hurricane. In the present state of the atmosphere these squalls may be constantly expected.

December 27, 1879

Stranger Things Have Happened.

Hold on, and you may walk over the sluggish animal up there yet.

The "Magnetic" Blaine; or, A Very Heavy "Load"-stone for the
Republican Party To Carry.

July 10, 1880

Boom ! ! !—So Near, and Yet so Far.

S.J.T. "By Jupiter! can't they understand a joke? Catch me believing in lightning-rods again!"

July 3, 1880

"A Midsummer-Night's Dream" Nomination.

THE QUEEN OF FAIRIES (COLUMBIA). "What angel wakes me from my flowery
bed? . . . Thou art as *wise* as thou art beautiful."—SHAKSPEARE.

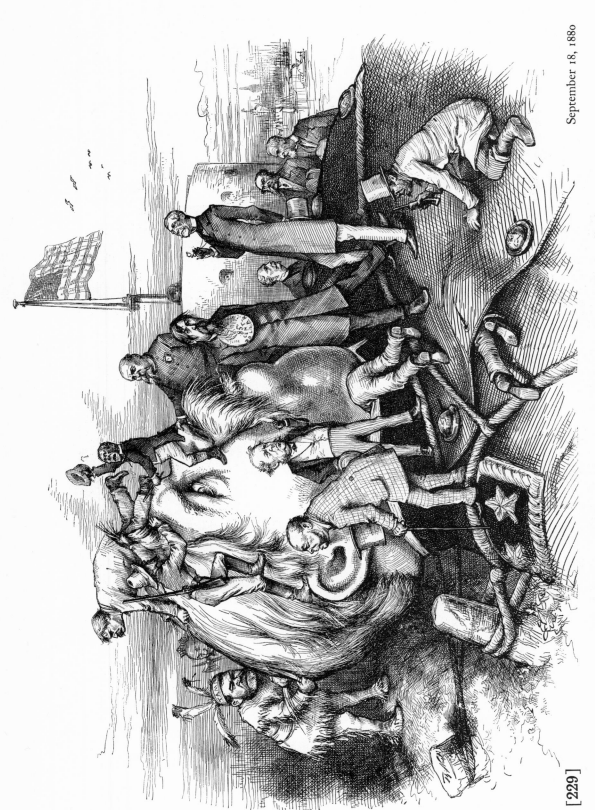

September 18, 1880

General Hancock Gulliver, How Do You Like It as Far as You've Got?

"I confess I was often tempted, while they were passing backward and forward on my body, to seize forty or fifty of the first that came in my reach, and dash them against the ground. But the remembrance of what I had felt, which probably might not be the worst they could do, and the promise of honor I made them, for so I interpreted my submissive behavior, soon drove out these imaginations. . . . However, in my thoughts I could not sufficiently wonder at the intrepidity of these diminutive mortals, who durst venture to mount and walk upon my body, while one of my hands was at liberty, without trembling at the very sight of so prodigious a creature as I must appear to them."

"THE LAST VESTIGE OF THE WAR LEGISLATION SHALL BE SWEPT FROM THE STATUTE BOOK."
SOLID SOUTH

"THE NATIONAL DEBT SHALL BE WIPED OUT."
SOLID SOUTH

"THE SOUTHERN DEBT MUST BE PAID SOMEHOW."
SOLID SOUTH

"ALL UNION SOLDIERS MUST GO."
SOLID SOUTH

SOLID (SOUTHERN) SENTIMENT.

ROBERT TOOMBS TO A FRIEND IN WASHINGTON.

"I AM as positive that HANCOCK will be elected as I am that there is a God in the heavens. You say that he is a Yankee. Well, I know that; and I know, too, that his sword has pierced the breast of many a gallant man in gray. But what are we to do? We can not put in one of our own men this time, and have to take a 'Yank.' That being the case, let us take one who is less 'blue-bellied' than the most of them. You may depend upon it, sir, that, 'Yank' or no 'Yank,' if elected, the old boys of the South will see that HANCOCK does the fair thing by them. In other words, he will run the machine to suit them, or they will run the thing themselves. They are not going to be played with any longer. If you hear any man say that HANCOCK can not carry all of the South, you may put him down as a d—— fool."

[230]

September 18, 1880

He Will Be Gulliver in the Hands of the Brobdingnagians.

BROBDINGNAG TOOMBS. "You may depend upon it, sir, that, 'Yank' or no 'Yank,' we will 'yank' you!"

[231]   May 14, 1881

Is There To Be a Power Behind the Throne?

December 10, 1881

From Grave to Gay.

March 19, 1881

Pan-Ic in Session.

Death to us (the people) and fun for them ("statesmen").

April 30, 1881

Citizen Beaver and "Statesman" Sloth.

May 21, 1881

Our Stumbling-Block.

While the Citizen Beaver labors for prosperity and good government, the "Statesman"
Sloth lies on his back and obstructs and destroys.

October 21, 1882

"Ay! There's the Rub!"—You Can't Change the Nature of the Animal.

July 18, 1885

What the Position of a President of the United States Really Is.

October 17, 1885

The End of Party Slavery.

PARTY SLAVE-DRIVER. "If we can't whip these Mugwumps into shape, *our occupation will be gone.*"

November 7, 1885

The Greatest Of American Intimidators North And South.

PRACTICAL POLITICIAN. "Vote as I dictate!"

[240]

Our System Of Feathering Nests Breeds Tweeds All Over The Land.

1822 — 1885.

THE HERO OF OUR AGE,——DEAD!

August 1, 1885

Acknowledgments and Bibliography

A number of people helped me to find my way over the unfamiliar terrain of art history. I want especially to thank my Brandeis colleague Creighton Gilbert and Professor Oliver Larkin of Smith College. Sheldon Meyer, Gerard S. Case, and Frederick Schneider of the Oxford University Press very imaginatively handled the editorial and makeup problems posed by this book. Miss Barbara Falcon capably coped with the typing. I want also to thank Mr. William R. Battey, Nast's great-grandson. I owe my customary debt of gratitude to my wife's sympathy, intelligence, and perception.

Goldfarb Library of Brandeis University graciously made available the set of *Harper's Weekly* from which the cartoons in this book were reproduced. My obligation to the efficient and obliging staff of that institution is very great.

In 1904 the critic and biographer Albert Bigelow Paine published *Th. Nast: His Period and His Pictures*. Paine wrote a solid, knowing, sympathetic study of Nast, on which I have relied heavily.

There is no substantial collection of Nast papers. The Huntington Library in San Marino, California, has a run of letters from the artist to his wife. The Rutherford B. Hayes Library in Fremont, Ohio, holds a few items, including some correspondence between Nast and David Ross Locke, the creator of Petroleum V. Nasby.

Nast's cartoons may best be viewed in their natural habitat the magazines, especially *Harper's Weekly*. The New York Public Library has a very large collection of mounted Nast drawings. The Library also has check lists of Nast's cartoons and of the books that he illustrated.

Besides contributing to the major pictorial magazines of his time, Nast illustrated a number of books. Among those that reveal something of his political viewpoint are Richard G. White, *The New Gospel of Peace* (New York, 1866); Anon. [Rev. Henry Williams], *The Fight at Dame Europa's School: Showing How the German Boy Thrashed the French Boy; and How the English Boy Looked On* (New York, 1871); David A. Wells, *Robinson Crusoe's Money; or, the Remarkable Financial Fortunes and Misfortunes of a Remote Island Community* (New York, 1876); and Rufus E. Shapley, *Solid for Mulhooly: A Political Satire* (Philadelphia, 1889).

In addition to Paine's book, the following works on Nast are useful: Arthur B. Maurice, "Thomas Nast and His Cartoons," *The Bookman*, XV (1902), 19-25; J. Chalmers Vinson, "Thomas Nast and the American Political Scene," *American Quarterly*, IX (Fall 1957), 337-44, and his *Thomas Nast: Political Artist* (Athens, Georgia, 1967); Lloyd Goodrich, "Thomas Nast," *The American-German Review*, I (March 1935), 12-16, 55; Elizabeth Luther Cary's discussion of Nast's art in the *New York Times*, July 9, 1933; Frank Weitenkampf, "Thomas Nast—Artist in Caricature," *New York Public Library Bulletin*, XXXVII (1933), 770-74; William Murrell, "Nast, Gladiator of the Political Pencil," *American Scholar*, V (1936), 472-85; John A. Kouwenhoven, "Thomas Nast as We Don't Know Him," *Colophon*, #2 (New Graphic Series) (1939); Ernest Knaufft, "Thomas Nast," *American Review of Reviews*, XXVII (January 1903), 31-35; and Walter Gutman, "An American Phenomenon," *Creative Art*, V (1929), 670-72.

Among the discussions of caricature that proved particularly helpful were: E. H. Gombrich and Ernst Kris, *Caricature* (London, 1940); Gombrich, "The Cartoonist's Armory," *South Atlantic Quarterly*, LXII (Spring 1963), 189-228; Kris, *Psychoanalytic Explorations in Art* (New York, 1952); Kris and Gombrich, "The Principles of Caricature," *British Journal of Medical Psychology*, XVII, Parts III and IV (1938), 319-42. I was helped too by Sigmund Freud's *Wit and Its Relations to the Unconscious* (New York, 1919), and Albert B. Paine, "The Origin of American Cartoon Symbols," *Harper's Weekly*, LII (Sept. 19, 1908), 11-12. The relevant European background is discussed in Mary D. George, *English Political Caricature; A Study of Opinion and Propaganda* (2 vol., Oxford, 1959), and Oliver W. Larkin, *Daumier, Man of His Time* (New York, 1966). Useful works on American graphic art are William Murrell, *A History of American Graphic Humor 1865-1938* (2 vol., New York, 1938), and Stephen Becker, *Comic Art in America* (New York, 1959).

The magazines to which Nast contributed are discussed in Frank L. Mott, *A History of American Magazines* (Cambridge, 1938—), Vol. II, III, and John H. Harper, *The House of Harper* (New York, 1912).

My interpretation of the relationship of Nast's art to his politics derives from a broader study of late nineteenth-century American public life on which I am now engaged. There is no better access to that relationship than a reading of *Harper's Weekly* during the years of Nast's flowering. The following historical works also were helpful: William F. Thompson, Jr., "Pictorial Propaganda and the Civil War," *Wisconsin Magazine of History*, XLVI (Autumn 1962), 21-31; James C. Austin, *Petroleum V. Nasby* (New York, 1965); Gunther P. Barth, *Bitter Strength: A History of the Chinese in the United States, 1850-1870* (Cambridge, 1964); Henry E. Fritz, *The Movement for Indian Assimilation, 1860-1890* (Philadelphia, 1963); Robert Cross, *The Emergence of Liberal Catholicism in America* (Cambridge, 1958); Alexander B. Callow, *The Tweed Ring* (New York, 1966); and Irwin Unger, *The Greenback Era* (Princeton, 1964).